Authentic
ALIGNMENT

Wise Women
Reveal the Secrets
to a Stellar Life

THRIVE Publishing
A Division of PowerDynamics Publishing, Inc.
San Francisco, California
www.thrivebooks.com

We Dedicate
This Book to You...

our reader;
a woman ready to discover the secrets
to a stellar life. You recognize the power
of learning from others as you embark
on your journey to authentic alignment.
We salute you for investing in yourself
and embracing the wisdom of others to achieve
fulfillment. We celebrate your commitment
to being the best you can be!

The Co-Authors of
Authentic Alignment

Table of Contents

Empowering Your Divine Life Purpose   **1**
Seven Keys to Loving Yourself and Fulfilling Your Life
By Rayna Lumbard, MA, LMFT, CHT

Discover the Steps to Loving Again After Divorce   **11**
By Christy Moore, BSN, MA, CPC

Obstacles Are Opportunities to Start Fresh   **21**
My Journey to Authentic Alignment
By Linda Ashley

Effectively Executing Your Company's Strategic Goals   **31**
By Paula E. Pacheco

Be Your Own Soul Massage™ Guide   **43**
Honor Authentic Presence and Expression
By Vicki Takeuchi Wynne, MSW, LMT

From No to Yes   **55**
Dare to Be Real
By Dot Claire, BSN, RN

Learning to Dream… Again   **67**
One Vision at a Time
By Maria Antonieta Gomez, AAS, BA

Get Your GLOW *On!*   **79**
By Katie Macks

Magical Moments   **89**
Key Practices to Welcome Bliss into Your Life
By Patti Martin, PsyD

Authentic Alignment with Your Feminine Resonance   101
Empowered Women in Harmony with Nature
By Shannon Murray, BS, BA, CMT

Don't Lose Heart in Tribulation   113
For It's Your Glory
By Kecia Hayslett, RN

The Art of Looking in the Other Direction   121
By Carla Carroll, NMLS, CA BRE

The Heart of Shame   131
By Michelle Gesky, CRC, CLC, CHC

More *Authentic Alignment*   142
Geographical Listings for *Authentic Alignment*   143
About THRIVE Publishing™   146
Other Books from THRIVE Publishing   148

Acknowledgements

Expressing appreciation is a key part of authentic alignment. Before we share our wisdom and experience with you, we have a few people to thank for turning our vision for this book into a reality.

This book is the brilliant concept of Caterina Rando, the founder of THRIVE Publishing™ and a respected business strategist and coach, with whom many of us have worked to grow our businesses. Working closely with many life coaches, consultants, and other professionals, she realized how valuable the knowledge they possessed would be to those people wanting to truly achieve authentic alignment. The result was putting our ideas into a comprehensive book on women's personal development.

Without Caterina's "take action" spirit, her positive attitude and her commitment to excellence, you would not be reading this book of which we are all so proud. She was supported by a dedicated team who worked diligently to put together the best possible book for you. We are truly grateful for everyone's stellar contribution.

To Karen Gargiulo, who served as the project manager and copy editor for this book, we appreciate your patient guidance, thoughtful advice, and genuine enthusiasm for our work, and we are truly grateful.

To Tammy Tribble and Noël Voskuil, our designers extraordinaire, who brought their creative talents to the cover and book layout, thank you both for your enthusiasm, problem solving and attention to detail throughout this project.

To Monique Cabading and Rua Necaise, who provided us with keen eyes and an elegant touch, thank you for your support and contribution and for making us read so perfectly on paper.

The Co-Authors of *Authentic Alignment*

Introduction

Congratulations! You have opened an incredible resource, packed with great ideas that can turn your life into a fulfilling, healthy and joyful adventure. You are about to discover how to *achieve authentic alignment.*

Personal development is much more than improving your talents. It is finding your identity and expanding your self-awareness, qualities and spirituality. It is a conscious pursuit of health, happiness and individual potential. It is building relationships with others and reaching out to offer your gifts.

The chapters in this book can help you discover proven ways to succeed in both your personal and your professional life. You will learn new ways to improve relationships and innovative techniques for leading with authenticity. You'll learn from amazing and inspiring individuals who have not only survived the challenges of life transitions but come out finding their genuine purposes in the world. We have joined together to give you highly effective strategies that take you from where you are to where you want to be. Some bits of advice are repeated in different chapters—that tells you how important that advice is!

It's all here—how-to's for identifying your values and belief patterns, changing your mindset, and tapping into your true calling. You'll learn ways to find your life's purpose and discover your passion. You'll discover motivation for leaving fear and destructive patterns behind, and how to be a leader in your own life.

All the co-authors you will meet in this book want you to have quality strategies and confident know-how to pursue your dreams! We have shared our best tips and proven guidelines to help you achieve the life you may never have thought possible.

To get the most out of this book, we recommend that you read through it once, cover to cover. Then go back and follow the tips that apply to you in the chapters most relevant to your current situation. Every improvement you make in yourself makes a difference in your life.

Your journey to a better you takes time, patience and determination. If you take action and apply the strategies, tips and tactics we share in these pages, you will reap many rewards. With our knowledge and your action, we are confident that you, too, will achieve *authentic alignment*.

To you and your continued success!

The Co-Authors of *Authentic Alignment*

Dear Gale & Mark
So wonderful Knowing You!

Empowering
Your Divine Life Purpose

SEVEN KEYS TO LOVING YOURSELF

AND YOUR FULFILLING LIFE

Enjoy your journey!

Rayna

By Rayna Lumbard, MA, LMFT, CHT

*B*eing authentic has everything to do with being ground-ed in who you truly are, not what you should be or do for approval or to just "survive." Most of us would agree that the best way to live fully is by having high self-esteem and being positive, passionate and purposeful. What motivates you to live your divine life purpose? What is "calling" you from a deeper place within yourself to serve your family, community and humanity? What keeps you "stuck" in old patterns to stay safe, yet not satisfied or excited about life?

DISCOVER WHAT YOUR SOUL IS CALLING YOU TO DO

1. Intuitive Knowing. Some of us know instinctively from early childhood why we are here and who our true self is.

2. Rewarding Experiences. Others discover their highest path of service through the joy of participating in and supporting worthy causes and activities that shape their conscious decisions.

3. Spiritual Crisis. When life throws you experiences that threaten your being and deeply shake your very core, you feel out of control, despair and pain. Even though you may receive comfort from loved ones and friends, the real "aha" moments come when you trust that God/Spirit guides you to your own answers within to elicit a break-through and transform your life.

I was a very energetic, loving, joyful child growing up with my parents and brother. Like most children, I was very sensitive to the energy in the house. I also felt responsible for making everyone happy so that I would feel safe and loved. This was an impossible role to take on. My happy, musical, fun-loving father had been ill since I was born. I made the core decision that it was my fault and that I had to take care of him. I thought I could save him and my world. My mother did not know how to be emotionally supportive. She chose to be the breadwinner to take care of us.

I was only nine when my father died and left me heartbroken and feeling alone. My world fell apart. I was the only one in the family not allowed to go to his funeral, which traumatized me long into adulthood. I fell into a deep depression and no one really reached out to me. I prayed for God to bless my father every day, which eased some of my pain and helped me feel his love and feel connected to the spirit world. Sometimes, when life got tough, I wanted to be with him so much I even wished that God would take me.

By age 12 I tried to enjoy my own musical talent by taking violin and piano lessons. However, I quit each time I started excelling musically. I think I subconsciously equated music with death. I was on a journey to discover what made me happy.

Although I struggled emotionally and socially into my twenties, I felt God's grace and began trusting that my life had meaning. For example, I had a number of serious car accidents over the years, yet I was never injured. And even during my darkest times, I felt empowered to keep going, not knowing where that would take me. I started experiencing divine inspiration and intervention. I knew my value and felt destined to use my talents and gifts to heal myself on all levels and fulfill my divine life purpose. I could choose to struggle or to take the higher road to health and wholeness.

My soul's calling is to share my unique healing gifts and to join others to make the world a more loving, compassionate, joyful, happy and abundant place to thrive.

As a student of life, holistic psychotherapist, wife and mother, I have learned to truly listen to and trust God's/Spirit's guidance. I have total faith that everything works in divine order in the universe and in our lives.

The keys to loving yourself and to inner success involve letting go and healing past destructive childhood programming. This unblocks your creativity to envision, feel, know and believe you can manifest your happy, healthy, loving, joyful and abundant future.

My intuitive gifts emerged strongly during junior high school. I focused on school and blossomed into being valedictorian of my class. I felt good about myself and continued to excel academically. Even though I had problems socially, I focused on my goal of becoming a dental hygienist.

SPIRITUAL AWAKENINGS—EMBODYING
LOVE FROM GOD/SPIRIT

When I was 23, I was in an unhealthy relationship and working very hard as a dental hygienist. I broke up with my boyfriend and went into a deep depression that landed me in a therapist's office.

By the next year, I had disabling pain in my fingers when I worked on dental patients. I was estranged from my mother and brother and felt so alone. My "aha" moment came when the doctor told me, "Rayna, there is nothing physically wrong with you!" A flash of lightning shot through me, and I instantly knew I was ready for a dramatic course correction. Spirit was telling me that it was time to do what I really wanted to do: become a marriage, family and child therapist. By loving myself unconditionally, my life fell into place more easily and effortlessly.

When I survived a ruptured appendix at 52, I felt another jolt that empowered me to take responsibility for my health, be more impactful, and live my purpose. I stepped up my spiritual practice by bringing in more love and light for accelerated healings and transformations. To this day I trust God's/Spirit's guidance to support me 100 percent in fulfilling my true life purpose—radiating love and light as a healing force for good on the planet.

I am so grateful for the higher energies that have been "channeling" through me for over thirty years. Being a psychospiritual therapist, coach and energy/sound healer brings me so much joy. It has given me the tools to enjoy my family and create balance. By saying "yes" to myself and life, I am the happiest and healthiest I have ever been.

I feel free to be myself, totally alive and authentically aligned with what lights me up creatively. This shows up in my career, relation-ships, health and just having fun. Getting past my musical blocks opened me up to enjoy singing in several community choirs. I love my ballroom dancing lessons and am having the time of my life. I love to travel to Hawaii a couple of times a year and swim with the dolphins. When I'm home meditating, I call them in and receive energy tune-ups from them.

By staying true to myself and aligning with my divine purpose, I receive "vibrational tune ups." My life experiences expand as I evolve spiritually each year. My life continually transforms when I heal old, painful childhood fears—false evidence appearing real—and negative subconscious programs—*I'm not lovable, not worthy, not important, not smart enough.*

I love connecting with people and inspiring them to face their fears and empower their divine life purpose. I had the pleasure of meeting Barbara, a technician who had recently moved to California from Canada. She left her husband and was depressed, unhappy in her career, and stuck in her relationships. I encouraged her to join my Laser-Light Coaching Circle and work with me privately.

Barbara set goals in alignment with her divine life purpose. Through this process she was able to finalize her divorce, quit her job, and become an energy healer herself. Over time she also manifested a wonderful soul partner in life and business!

Barbara told me that my nurturing presence and loving guidance inspired and encouraged her to face her fears, to listen to and trust herself. She said, "The life purpose meditation gave me the most powerful messages from my soul."

Are you personally and professionally fulfilled in your life right now? Why or why not? Take a moment to connect with your heart. Imagine what your life will look like and how you will feel when you deeply honor your innate talents and gifts. Set your intention to be who you truly are by healing whatever stops you from living your divine life purpose. Commit to taking action and see what happens. You have the power to co-create with God/Spirit. Now let's get to work!

SEVEN KEYS TO LOVING YOURSELF TO EMPOWER AND FULFILL
YOUR DIVINE LIFE PURPOSE

1. Take responsibility for your life and health.

Everything happens to you for a reason and in divine timing for your soul growth and transformation. You have free will to decide how to react or respond to your circumstances. Once you accept what you draw into your life, you can take charge of changing it. The universe—God/Spirit—supports what you think and feel about everything, positive or negative.

"There are no victims, only volunteers."
**—Eleanor Roosevelt, American former First Lady,
politician, diplomat and activist**

2. Take good care of your body temple.

Being healthy is your natural state of being. You can even override your genetics through positive thoughts and habits. Eating healthy foods and drinking pure water supports your body's vitality. You can *prevent* imbalances or dis-eases more easily than healing them. Engage in what exercise, movement or activities feel good to your body. Pay attention when your body talks to you—or screams at you! Say this affirmation: *Health is my true wealth.*

3. Be aware of what causes your stress.

Become more conscious of tension in your body and what you think and feel that causes your stress. You may do this on your own or work with a practitioner to discover the stress triggers in your life. You may notice feeling anxious or low energy, have a physical complaint like a stomach or backache, or negative self-talk. Evaluate what is happening in your job or relationship that is causing your upset. Keep a journal of what is happening in your life and brainstorm ways to *be the change* you want to see. Know that you can take charge of staying centered and calm.

4. Transform negative beliefs and emotional pain.
When you are ready to get "unstuck" and manifest your divine life purpose, you will attract an experienced and gifted therapist to clear your issues with you on a deeper heart and soul level. Trust that you will be supported on your journey back in time to painful experiences, most likely from your childhood. For example, if your dad left the family, you may have created a negative perception of yourself—that you are unlovable. To heal deep wounds, you will love and nurture your inner child and heal your heart by expressing all your painful emotions as they come up. Now you can make new, powerful, positive decisions to replace the negative ones. You will create a new, positive scene based on what you wanted to have happened. Your mind and feelings respond as if the new scene is real. Now your inner child can heal from the trauma, grow up feeling loved, and become the empowered adult.

**5. Open your heart to create harmonious relationships
with positive, like-minded, supportive people.**
Having high self-esteem means opening your loving heart and being compassionate without taking on others' issues and pain. Even if you trigger their upset, you are not responsible for their feelings or happiness. When you focus on the positive and feel happy and peaceful within, you attract like-minded people who are open to creating win-win situations. It is the law of attraction in action. Use it to your advantage by letting your inner light shine when you meet people.

6. Commit yourself to a spiritual practice, be joyful and have fun!
Being spiritual is as easy as feeling loving, grateful or appreciative. You can focus on deepening your breath, being still, and listening

deeper for inner guidance. Spending time in nature is a great way to commune with your spirit, lighten you up, and have fun. You have unique, creative gifts of the spirit and innate intelligence. You know how to share them joyfully from your heart. Balance your life, laugh, and know that you are one with God/Spirit.

"Creativity is intelligence having fun."
—Albert Einstein, German-born theoretical physicist and philosopher of science

7. Fulfill your divine life purpose by being your authentic self.
Being your authentic self means being grounded in who you truly are, not what you or others think you should be. Fulfilling your divine life purpose means that your highest, authentic self directs your life. You become an original work of art as you present yourself as honest, natural and believable. Empower your divine purpose by saying yes to yourself, your dreams and your passions. Realize what a gift you are to the planet with no ego attachment.

To live authentically and in harmony with your higher life purpose, fill out this statement naming your highest authentic self (metaphor), how you express your soul's nature, and your divine life purpose— your impact, contribution, gift or service to the planet statement.

Example: I am the bright sun that warms and illuminates the planet for people to manifest their highest and best selves.

I am the _____ (metaphor)
that _____ (soul's expression)
for _____ or so that people
_____.
(impact/contribution/gift/or service to others and the world)

Affirmation: I, _____ (your name) am ready to live and express my highest authentic self in harmony with my divine life purpose. I am committed to being who I truly am and sharing my highest contribution to humanity.

Let go of your fears and doubts. Appreciate and develop your skills, gifts and talents. Open up to the natural flow of abundance and enjoy yourself. When you think of what you do as being of service, you feel wonderful making a greater impact and contribution to the world. Transform your life for *good!*

Rayna Lumbard, MA, LMFT, CHT
InnerSuccess Transformations
Mind/Body/Spirit Therapy and Healing

408-605-9195
rayna@innersuccess.com
www.innersuccess.com

Rayna Lumbard is a licensed marriage and family therapist, master hypnotherapist, psychospiritual energy/sound healer, and life/business coach. She created *InnerSuccess Transformations,* powerful tools to accelerate the healing of the mind, body, spirit and emotions. She has thirty years of experience supporting her clients to relax and transform their lives. Rayna sees individuals, couples and families in her office on a creek in Saratoga, California, and also works intuitively with clients on the phone and through distant healing.

Rayna guides you to release negative core beliefs, painful emotions, blocked energy, and traumas holding you back from reaching your goals and dreams. Her positive support helps you manifest loving relationships, successful careers, vibrant health, and a fulfilling, purposeful life. She also facilitates transformational play shops including The Law of Attraction in Action, Seven Keys to Vibrant Health and Life Wealth, and Healing Energetically with the Dolphins.

In addition to her therapy career, Rayna is the co-founder of The Awareness Network, a spiritually-based networking organization which has been meeting weekly for twenty years. She has written numerous publications, is a contributing author to *The Power of Miracle Thinking,* published in 2008 by Author One Stop and *GodBumps: Connecting to the Spiritual World through the Five Senses,* published by Pfaffle & Pfaffle in 2010, and appears on many TV and radio programs.

Discover the Steps to Loving Again After Divorce

By Christy Moore, BSN, MA, CPC

Going through divorce is one of the most difficult experiences. After going through two divorces, I knew I needed to take a closer look at myself and the part I played. I was devastated. Still, I did the work which liberated me from that past and catapulted me forward so that I could be in a loving and committed marriage today.

It does not matter if you are the person who initiated the divorce. You still experience a sense of loss. Now what? In today's society, it is common knowledge that the divorce rate is high. We are not formally taught about relationships or marriage. We model our ideas of love and romance after movie characters, or princes and princesses who go on to live happily ever after. Truth be told, many of us spend more time and energy on planning our weddings than we do on ourselves or the quality of our relationships. After a divorce, you have the opportunity to do things differently.

> *"Choose your life's mate carefully. From this one decision*
> *will come 90 percent of all your happiness or misery."*
> **—H. Jackson Brown Jr., American author**

In this chapter, I share three steps you can take to be successful at loving again after divorce. Once I learned and implemented the steps, I was empowered. I approached finding love after my own divorce entirely from a new, clear and joyful perspective. These three steps are what enabled me to love myself, love my life, and be open to loving another. With these steps I updated my attitude, sharpened my skills, created a vision for new love, and took action. It worked!

My intention for you is that when you begin your journey back to loving yourself, loving your life and loving another, these steps will support you and make the experience smoother, easier and more fun.

STEP 1: UPDATE YOUR ATTITUDE
WHAT IS ATTITUDE?

The Merriam-Webster® dictionary defines attitude as *"a feeling or way of thinking that affects a person's behavior."* It can also be described as a bias, frame of mind and opinion.

WHY DOES ATTITUDE MATTER?

After divorce, it is understandable that your attitude toward men, love, and relationships is less than positive. As a result of this attitude, you may come across as unfriendly, closed, or having a negative vibe. However, to begin the journey back to loving yourself, loving your life and loving another, a change in attitude is a great first step you can take.

Your attitude is the tint that colors everything you say and do. It speaks before you do! If you spend any time around teenagers, you understand what I mean. When that teen has a negative attitude, it comes across loud and clear no matter what he or she says or does. You see it in his body language or hear it in her voice. The attitude acts like a filter which distorts the communication and connection, and, consequently, influences and impacts the relationship negatively.

"Who you are speaks so loudly I can't hear what you're saying."
—**Ralph Waldo Emmerson, American poet and philosopher**

If you apply that same principle to yourself, can you imagine how having a negative attitude about yourself, men, love and relationships "speaks" so loudly that no one can hear what you are saying? You are actually giving off mixed signals that can be confusing to others. If you only change your actions, your appearance, or what you say, without making a change in your attitude, there is a disconnect between what you say you want and what your body language communicates.

HOW DO I UPDATE MY ATTITUDE?

One way you can begin to transform your attitude is to ask yourself empowering questions that are designed to change your thinking. The payoff for changing your thinking is that your new attitude empowers you to show up for love from a place of joy, optimism and openness. You send a signal to the world that says *Yes! I have a new attitude and I am really ready for love!* Your body language and your actions are congruent.

Empowering questions are open-ended, exploratory questions intended to help clarify your point of view, search for new under-standing, and introduce you to different options for consideration.

In a journal or a notebook, write down and answer the following questions:
- What is really getting in the way of my thinking?
- What is another way to look at this so I can move on?

• What type of relationship do I want to experience now?
• What really excites me about that?
• What would it take for that to happen?

Know that changing the way you think about something is a catalyst for raising your energy and updating your attitude. Now that you know what your thoughts are, you can choose more empowering ones. Use the answers to these questions as a starting point to make the adjustments that will tint your life in a whole new bright, bold and loving way.

STEP 2. UPDATE YOUR RELATIONSHIP SKILLSET
SKILLSET DEFINED

I love the way the Merriam-Webster dictionary defines *skillset:* "*The group of skills that a person has acquired in order to perform a task or job.*" In the realm of finding love after divorce, your skillset includes your behaviors and the physical actions you take that are intended to move you toward finding love again.

WHY DOES UPDATING MY SKILLSET MATTER?

Whether you were married for five years or twenty years, now that you are single again, a lot may have changed for you. Some questions people ask are *Where do people meet nowadays? How safe is using the Internet? What do these text messages really mean? Am I being asked out?*

Other areas of concern you may have are how to have a decent conversation, when to include your children, and how to look *your* best—not someone else's idea of your best. Taking an inventory of your skillset is another powerful step that signals you are ready for a new chapter in your life and a new love. After going through a divorce, you may decide that you no longer want to repeat certain actions and behaviors because they no longer serve you. Now is the time to be aware of what did not work and make the changes.

I compare updating your relationship skillset to updating your skills for a new job or career change. Many of us would not think twice about doing whatever was required to be successful in a new job. Think about finding love again after divorce in the same way. If you want a new and better relationship, you will have to put in the work.

HOW DO I UPDATE MY SKILLSET?

When you take an inventory of your skillset, you are taking a bold step. Awareness is the first step in being able to make a change. If you are not certain where to begin, try beginning with the end in mind. What is your ideal image of the skills needed to meet the type of person and have the type of relationship you desire?

In my quest to upgrade my own skills, I looked at where I was and decided where I wanted to go. There was a huge gap and I took small steps. Eventually I got to a place where my skills had improved. I kept moving in the direction of my desire. I practiced the behaviors and took the action that I knew would lead me to success.

Here is a process that you can use to identify and begin to upgrade your skillset. For this process you can also use your journal or a simple spiral bound notebook.

1. List all of the skills you think would be beneficial to have in order to be successful in finding love again. Include inner skills like changing limiting beliefs, letting go of the past, and creating a vision for new

love, as well as outer skills such as being able to set up an online dating profile and knowing where to meet available and eligible men.

2. On a scale of one to ten, where one means you do not have the skill now and ten means you totally have the skill, go over your list and rate each skill as it is today.

3. List all the skills you would like to develop, change or improve.

4. Choose the top three skills you want to develop, change or improve by two or three points within one to three months.

5. Write up a plan for developing, changing or improving the skill by just a few notches. For example, if you rated your wardrobe a four, what would it take to raise the rating to a six?

6. In your plan, include what you will do, when you will start, who could help you be accountable for making the changes, and how you will measure your success. What will it look like when your skills have improved by two or three points?

You do not need to make gigantic leaps to be successful. Making a few smaller strides can yield big results. This process may take some time; therefore, be gentle with yourself. Update your plan often with your successes. Soon, you will look back at where you started and see all that you did, and you will see how far you have come on your journey back to finding love after divorce.

STEP 3. UPDATE YOUR VISION
WHAT DOES VISION MEAN?

The Merriam-Webster® dictionary defines vision as *"something that you imagine; a picture that you see in your mind."* The *something* I am referring to in this chapter is a new, loving, conscious, committed relationship or marriage.

WHY DOES HAVING A VISION MATTER?

Creating a vision for a new love and relationship is not just about crafting a collage from magazine cutouts and pasting them in your journal. That is a small fraction of the power of creating a vision. The real power comes from you being able to visualize and feel a whole new experience. This new vision will then influence your attitude, beliefs, behaviors, actions and skills.

Imagine you are planning a trip from California to New York without a map. You have no information about road conditions, alternate routes, where you will stop to eat and sleep, or what you will see along the way. How does that vision make you feel? Now imagine that you do have a map and you know the way you want to go and what to do if there was to be a detour. Knowing where you want to go, you can then imagine all of the places you may want to visit on your way to New York. How different is this vision? Did you see more details? Did it feel more fun?

Having a vision supports you in not only reaching your goal, but also in being more flexible about what happens along the way so that you are not derailed. Your vision inspires you and positively influences your attitude and your behaviors, just as having a new attitude and behaviors supports your vision. It is a win-win-win.

HOW DO I UPDATE MY VISION?

One of the keys to creating a vision is being willing to move on from your past so that your vision focuses only on what you want. If the vision you are creating is not taking you where you want to go, perhaps you are focusing on what you do *not* want. For example, if you focus on finding someone who is *not* selfish, *not* into football, *not* a smoker, or *not* taller or shorter than six feet, then you are more likely to notice and attract what you do *not* want.

> *"If you don't know where you are going,*
> *any road will get you there."*
> **—Lewis Carroll, English author**

The first step is getting clear about the kind of relationship you desire now. To set the tone for this exercise, find a comfortable and relaxing place where you can think and write without interruption for a couple of hours. Put on some music, light a candle, or go outside to your favorite place in nature. The idea is that you want to be free from distractions, be relaxed and be free to imagine and write as much as you would like.

For this exercise, you are going to write yourself a letter, dated one year from today, as if you were writing to a friend you love and trust, someone you have not spoken to in quite a while. You are eager to update her about what has been going on in your life over the past year and how so many wonderful things have happened, including being in love again.

In your letter, share about your new love. Include every detail about what you did to transform yourself into the type of woman who was ready, willing and able to get back out there, confidently empowered. Talk about your change in attitude, your new skills, what you had to do to prepare for love. Include all the qualities you had to develop, what changes you made inside of yourself, how you took charge and decided upon your relationship must-haves and deal-breakers. Talk about your adventures in dating and how much fun you have been having. Tell her all about your new life, love, what the relationship feels like, and how much joy it brings you.

When you complete your letter, be sure to save it. You will read it aloud to yourself when you wake up in the morning and before you go to bed. You may want to record yourself reading it so you can play it back privately. This exercise anchors the energy and enthusiasm of your vision.

You may also want to make a collage and include imagery and words that represent your vision of you with your new love. You can include images symbolizing shared experiences, travel, fun, romance and blended families. The sky is the limit. This is your vision. You have permission to make it as fun and exciting as you want.

TIME TO TAKE ACTION

Loving after divorce is a journey and an adventure. Yes, the journey can be full of potholes, detours and dead-end streets. When your vision of loving again is backed up with a new attitude and new skills, you will be well equipped to navigate whatever obstacles you encounter. If you were driving on your way to see your favorite band perform and you came to a dead-end street, would you turn around and go home? No! You would find a way to get there because you had a vision for what you wanted to do and nothing would stop you. When you implement the three steps of updating your attitude, skillset and vision, you will know who you are, what you want, and how to travel the road that will take you there.

Christy Moore, BSN, MA, CPC
Moore Joy Coaching
Certified Professional Coach, speaker
and workshop facilitator

310-936-6193
christy@moorejoycoaching.com
www.moorejoycoaching.com

Christy Moore, BSN, MA, CPC, is a Certified Strategic Attraction™ Coach whose mission is to teach divorced women how to attract their perfect soul-mate relationship. Her own experience with being divorced and learning what it takes to be happily single and then be successful in love was the catalyst for launching her business.

Like many divorced women, Christy discovered that traveling the road back to loving herself and her life, and being open to new love, was paved with detours and roadblocks. She persevered and reached her destination. Her biggest wins occurred when she found the courage to align her desires, choices and behaviors with attracting and manifesting the relationship that was perfect for her. Through coaching, speaking, online courses, and workshops, Christy empowers women to create their own Strategic Attraction Plan™ so they can attract and manifest their perfect relationship, dinner date or soul mate.

Christy is a native Californian and resides in Los Angeles with her husband. She has two sons and a grandson. She is excited about supporting women everywhere to love their lives and love another again. *Email me at christy@moorejoycoaching.com for the free workbook based on this chapter.*

Obstacles Are Opportunities to Start Fresh

MY JOURNEY

TO AUTHENTIC ALIGNMENT

By Linda Ashley

 have had a lifetime filled with the highs and lows that come with living. I have given myself over to the dreams of others.

Life was easy in my early years. I was born into a loving and successful family. We were upper middle class entrepreneurial Americans living in the suburbs of the San Francisco Bay Area.

While in college in San Francisco, I met and married my first husband. We became parents a little over a year later. Then our marriage fell apart. Enter the first big obstacle of my young life.

I was a single mom with a baby boy. I had no job; an obstacle I attacked with panic and fear. My son and I moved in with my parents, and soon I found a job in accounting working for a CPA.

My mom had been diagnosed with cancer—enter the second big obstacle in my life. Sometimes obstacles are there to put you in exactly the right place at the right time. Living at home allowed us to spend the last year of my mom's life with her.

My life revolved around my family and work. I did not notice that the authentic *me* was missing.

A couple of years later, I met and married my second husband. We were both entrepreneurs. In our early years, we owned a photography studio and a bridal salon. Then, in our forties, we changed course and opened a technical service company that serviced the graphic arts and photo processing industry in the Silicon Valley, as well as a travel agency.

Over the years, we faced many obstacles, challenges and opportunities together. Although I thought at the time that I was living my authentic life, I later realized that I was still marching to the drum of other people's ideas of what was right for me.

GREAT OPPORTUNITIES

In 2003, my husband was jogging and had a massive heart attack. His death was my biggest obstacle yet. I closed his business and kept my travel agency. I also began a marketing coaching company, since I had been marketing for our own businesses for years.

In 2004, I was approached about taking on the role of president and CEO of the Newark Chamber of Commerce, a position I really enjoyed. A few months later, I closed the travel agency.

A decade later, in 2014, it was time for me to retire. I had intended to ramp up my marketing business; however, I started to realize it was no longer serving me. Plus, I knew that I did not have it in my DNA to retire as others had encouraged me to do. How would I get from doing the things I loved as president and CEO to retirement my way, while still doing what I loved? I would like to share with you what I discovered on my journey.

12 TIPS TO AUTHENTIC ALIGNMENT

TIP #1: START AT THE BEGINNING

Do not turn down opportunities to meet people. Someone just may have the answers you are looking for. I had no clue about what I wanted to do with myself. A friend invited me to an event called *Time to Thrive* by Caterina Rando. I agreed to attend just to support my friend and found that I was instantly drawn to Caterina. I was definitely in the right place at the right time.

TIP #2: LOOK FOR AHA MOMENTS

Since retiring from the Chamber, I had been trying to fit my creative self into a 9-to-5 schedule. No! I was a night owl. My creative time is well after midnight. My first aha moment came within the first two minutes of the *Time to Thrive* presentation. I heard Caterina say, "Guess what, Ladies? When you are in business for yourself, you are the boss. You set where, when and how you want to do your business!" That was a huge aha moment for me.

TIP #3: EDUCATE YOURSELF

Look for opportunities to absorb new skills and knowledge that support you. I decided I needed to spend more time around Caterina and learn from her. I signed up for her next two events. The first day brought me another huge aha moment: Surprise! I did not know it all. I discovered that there was so much I had to learn. I must have had sixty items on my action list by the end of the day. That night in my hotel room, I sat down with a fresh pad of paper, my notes and a glass of wine. With background music on the radio, I started building my new business.

I started a new list about who I was and what I wanted to do with my life. The key is to just write—do not filter. Do not worry about spelling, complete sentences or even making sense. My final list was several pages long and included notes from my day with Caterina, what I loved about the work I had done over the last forty years, and what I had loved about my work at the Chamber. About 3:00 a.m., I turned over the tablet and went to bed. The next morning when I looked at my list, I realized I had created an entirely new business that would serve the authentic me!

TIP #4: BE FLEXIBLE AND OPEN TO CHANGE

A key to starting fresh is to be flexible and open to changing your way of thinking and doing business. Having been an entrepreneur for over forty years, I found it easy to fall into the "I've always done it that way" trap. Do not do that! Every day new ideas are developed. We had no computers, Internet availability or cell phones when I started out. It is important that you are willing to not only be open to changes, but to fully embrace them.

TIP #5: DO THE RESEARCH

If your plan is to start a business, then it is important that you thoroughly research the possibilities, including finding those that have already successfully done what you want to do. How did they get started? Is their ideal client your ideal client? How did they market their business? How long did it take them to be profitable? One of the areas I am researching for my business is seniors who want to retire their own way—not the way many are told they should. Whether you retire to watch TV or play golf or start a new business, it is your choice. To live authentically, you need to choose for yourself.

TIP #6: FIND A GREAT MENTOR OR COACH

You cannot do it all alone. A great mentor or coach will work with you to think outside the box. That person will connect you to others who can help you succeed. Find someone with a background in your field. As my mentor/coach Caterina Rando says, "Find someone who will hold a bigger vision for you than you hold for yourself."

TIP #7: FIND A COMMUNITY OR NETWORK

A community is a group of like-minded people who share common attitudes, interests and goals. One of its big advantages is discovering you are not in it alone. Communities come in many forms, from mentoring communities like Caterina's and mine, to chambers of commerce, to business associations, to mastermind groups. I encourage you to find one. However, do not join everything available. Join where you can serve and be served. Participate.

TIP #8: FIND SOMEONE TO HOLD YOU ACCOUNTABLE

If you are a solo-preneur, it is vital to have an accountability coach or partner. When you work alone, it is too easy to procrastinate on certain tasks. I suggest you work with someone who will encourage you to do what you say you will do to grow your business.

TIP #9: ENLIST PROFESSIONAL SUPPORT FOR MARKETING

You cannot do everything yourself! Do what is the best use of your time. If you are a new entrepreneur, you may not have the finances to hire an assistant. However, you may find that you can afford to hire a virtual assistant on a project-by-project basis. While your virtual assistant is adding business cards to your database, you are doing sales calls or other income-producing activities.

TIP #10: WATCH YOUR FINANCIAL INVESTMENTS

Negative cash flow is the biggest obstacle new business owners face. It can derail your plans in an instant. Do not fall into the pie-in-the-sky syndrome. As an entrepreneur, you are bombarded with offers in your email every day. They come in the form of marketing, training, conferences and other great deals. Many, including me, have bought into these programs and then never fully utilized them. It is like throwing money down the drain. It would be nice to start a business with a lot of money in the bank. The reality is that for most of us, it does not happen that way. Make a plan and stick to it!

TIP #11: JOIN A MASTERMIND GROUP

A great mastermind group brings a small number of entrepreneurs—my ideal number is four to seven people—together to think outside the box for one another. As a member, be open to suggestions, offer ideas, keep information confidential and take notes. It is important to have rapport with the facilitator and the other members. Share the suggestions you receive with your mentor. This can provide an excellent opportunity to expand your business.

TIP #12: BE LOUD AND PROUD ABOUT WHAT YOU DO

No one is better at being loud and proud about your business than you are! As children, we were taught not to brag. However, when it comes to business, your prospects and clients need to know that you can serve them well. You must tell them about your successes in any way you can. On your website, in your newsletter and in social media, post your education, conferences and seminars you attend, awards you win, and most important, testimonials from satisfied clients. Beginning with your very first client, ask for a testimonial and then tell the world!

LESSONS LEARNED FROM OBSTACLES

Along the road to living authentically and succeeding in business, I learned many lessons about how to turn obstacles into opportunities. Here are seven lessons I learned that can help you, too.

- **Disappointments and stress are only temporary.** Take a deep breath and realize obstacles are only momentary setbacks that you can—and will—find a way to get past. With the right attitude, you may discover something even better than what you had.
- **You are stronger than you thought.** This is not the first obstacle you have faced. It will not be your last. Reflect on past experiences to help you face this one.
- **The right support can create positive change.** Rely on family, friends, business partners and associates, mental health professionals, business mentors and coaches, or anyone you know who will help you change an obstacle into an opportunity.
- **Think outside the box.** Have a mastermind session with yourself. Ask yourself what you would do if image, money or failure did not exist.
- **Take care of yourself.** Get extra rest, eat well, exercise, play more and have "me" time. Read motivational books. The unconditional love from a cherished pet can also do wonders when you are stressed.
- **Change your mindset, change your life.** Live from where you are going, not from where you have been. There is a saying that suggests that your personality takes on that of the five people you hang out with the most. Their attributes become yours—and so do their vices. The quickest way to become a negative person is to be around negative people. Do not let negativity into your life. Letting go is a huge stress releaser.
- **Help someone else get what they want and you will get what you want.** Helping others feels good!

In the end, it is not the obstacles in life that define you. What does define you and allows you to be in authentic alignment is how you deal with those obstacles. Handled well, you will build your self-esteem, confidence, knowledge and abilities to become the authentic person you were meant to be.

WOMEN OF A CERTAIN AGE
OWN AUTHENTIC ALIGNMENT

It has been pointed out in the media that the youth culture often discards women when they reach a certain age. I think that is a flawed concept. It is not the youth culture that discards people of a certain age; it is we, the women of that certain age, who can easily do it to ourselves with limiting beliefs related to age and retirement. Age does not matter unless we make it matter! You see, as a woman who was part of the sixties hippie generation, I never believed those limiting beliefs in the first place. Yet they were drilled into my head by well-meaning people who wanted me to live their version of retirement. There was a constant struggle about what was possible for me at this stage of my life. As women of a certain age, we must release the limiting beliefs of others and embrace the powerful, limitless beliefs within ourselves.

"Your time is limited, so don't waste it living someone else's life. Don't be trapped by dogma—which is living with the results of other people's thinking. Don't let the noise of others' opinions drown out your own inner voice. And most important, have the courage to follow your heart and intuition."
—**Steve Jobs, American entrepreneur, marketer, inventor, and co-founder, chairman, and CEO of Apple® Inc.**

Authentic women of a certain age are not living shallow lives. We are living vibrant lives where we respect, support, and learn from each other. We naturally mentor and do the same for young entrepreneurs.

It is our responsibility to help other women of any age, and especially of a certain age, do the same. Authenticity and a joyful life happened when I let go of everyone else's plan for me and began to live my life and my retirement—my way! Let's do it!

MY AUTHENTIC ALIGNMENT

My baby boy is now 46 years old, a husband, a dad to two awesome daughters and a full-time musician. The lesson he learned from me was that to live authentically, you must live your dream. He is living his dream. The tragic loss of my husband led me to the opportunity and joy of sharing a home with my son and his family. I have now found my authentic self in retirement my way. I am living my dream.

Start right this minute! Make this your year to find your authentic alignment, whether you are just starting out in business, a senior looking to retire your way, or at any point in between. You can make your dream a reality.

Linda Ashley
Business Strategist
Keeping your entrepreneurial dream alive and flourishing at any age

510-919-3696
linda@ashleybiz.com
www.ashleybiz.com

Linda Ashley follows the tradition of her entrepreneurial family. She has been self-employed for more than forty years, a decade of which included serving as the president and CEO of the Newark Chamber of Commerce. Linda became the "go-to" person for advice and help with business opportunities and challenges. She is a mastermind facilitator, speaker, author, connector, blogger, trainer, event planner, retreat facilitator, seminar and workshop leader, and director for *Today's Innovative Woman Magazine.*

Linda has received numerous awards for her work over the years, including the *Rising Star Award* from Thriving Women in Business, *Certificate of Special Congressional Recognition* from the U.S. House of Representatives, a *California Legislature Resolution Commendation* from the 25th Assembly District, and a *Commendation for Initiative, Knowledge, and Work Ethic* from the Office of the Mayor of Newark.

Linda attended San Jose State and Golden Gate University, majoring in business administration and accounting. She shares a home with her son, Jim, daughter-in-law, Lisa, and two granddaughters, Kirsten and Emily.

Discover your path to Authentic Alignment! Schedule your complimentary mentoring session with Linda at www.ashleybiz.com.

Effectively Executing Your Company's Strategic Goals

By Paula E. Pacheco

When I was in the corporate world, large companies would periodically embrace many different strategic goals for achieving success. While these goals were certainly beneficial, they often provided minimal impact except to create employee discontent. Where I worked, even after all the meetings, pep rallies and paraphernalia—a leather bound book entitled *Strategic Goals* was created in support of the new endeavor— yet nothing ever changed in the organization, except the wasted time spent watching sleep-inducing PowerPoint® slides.

The problem lay in the fact that no one in a leadership position knew how to convert strategic goals into specific, executable action steps to take in order to reach those goals. The executive committee would hand over the leather book to the senior staff and leave the execution of the goals to them. The senior staff would hand over the leather book to the vice presidents, who would hand it over to the managerial staff, who would glance at the book, and leave it on a shelf, never to be looked at again.

Unfortunately, a company's success is no longer measured by years, but by quarters, and the biggest obstacle to success is the absence of strategic execution.

For any business to be successful, it must have a culture of execution. This means that all employees can successfully execute all of their daily decisions, knowing exactly how their decisions are linked to the success of the strategic goals of the business.

"Power is the ability to get things done."
—Rosabeth Moss Kanter, American director/chair
of Harvard University Advanced Leadership Initiative

Strategic goals are doomed to fail if you do not engage the employees who will be most affected by them. I was hired as an operations manager by a Fortune 500 company going through a third reorganization and a new CEO. The staff was obviously nervous and very frustrated. At the end of my second week on the job, I was given a 45-page process improvement plan written by an outside consulting company. This report listed forty process changes that, once implemented throughout the department, were supposed to help produce the goals stated in the new CEO's strategic plan.

I was never told exactly what those strategic goals were, except that they would improve the company. So I rolled up my sleeves, read the report, and excitedly got to work.

Common sense told me that I must first speak to the experts of these processes—the staff. I sat down with the first of about 25 employees to discuss the changes that needed to be implemented. By the time I had spoken to the third employee, I realized that the consultants had only asked these employees how they performed their jobs. With only that information, the consultants went off and created the process changes they felt would ensure that the department would be doing its part in reaching the company's strategic goals. The consultants never asked the employees if they had any process-improvement ideas or solutions, or if the consultants' recommendations were even feasible. Many were not.

I spent the next 18 months, sometimes spending 12- to 15-hour days, working with employees, soliciting their suggestions and ideas, tweaking, revising, and sometimes completely changing the improvement plan so it could be executable.

Unbeknownst to me, engaging the employees' input in these changes caused them to take ownership of the revised changes, work harder to ensure successful execution, and significantly improved their attitudes.

For the rest of my management career, I never instituted changes without first discussing those changes, as well as organizational goals, with my staff. They have the solutions and usually much better ideas at reaching the goals.

COMMUNICATION AND CONFIDENCE

While working on my first strategic project, I unknowingly began learning about strategic execution. I also learned a lot about successful business communication. When it comes down to it, isn't everything about communication?

I discovered that for successful change, you first must gain feedback from those affected. You also need clear communication on purpose, goals, benefits, roles, responsibilities, rewards and consequences. By involving employees in the change process, you gain new insights, ideas and cogent suggestions as well as gaining employees who want to make meaningful contributions to their work life.

When I brought this new knowledge forward into my career, executing any kind of project I was involved in became so much simpler and easier, and it was financially successful for the company as well.

From then on, I read a myriad of business books and took business classes, including those on strategy and execution. Up until a few years ago, I never realized that strategy execution is a skill that only a small percentage of companies perform well. I only knew that I loved it! Believe me; I did not start out my career wanting to learn how to execute strategy. I am extremely grateful for where my initial experience at that Fortune 500 company has led me.

This strategy execution skill has allowed me to successfully take on diverse projects that I found interesting and challenging. It has enhanced endeavors of various sizes that involved all kinds of strategic initiatives or changes. For me, having the confidence to take on different projects was personally challenging and great fun. As an extra benefit, this gave me more diverse skills to add to my repertoire. Looking back now, I would not have it any other way.

COMPANY-WIDE AUTHENTIC COMMUNICATION IS KEY

To be an effective leader at any level, from front-line supervisor to CEO, I encourage you to find out everything you can about your department, your division and your company. Learn what your staff is doing and the reasons behind their actions. The higher you go up the chain, the more filtered the information you will receive. Therefore, it is best to personally find out what is really going on in the day-to-day world of your employees. Walk around and talk to your employees in simple English—no business speak. Get to know them. Even more important, let them get to know you. Always be honest and genuine. Talk about what is truly on your mind. Ask probing questions. Share your knowledge at every opportunity. Follow through on all of your commitments. This is being an authentic and trusted leader, and it will lead you to self-satisfaction and success.

When you begin encouraging employees to communicate with you, you begin learning about your organization's ability to execute. Since your employees are the experts in their domain, they have the information necessary to understand the front-line impact of strategic decisions. This is crucial information that executive management is usually unaware of. Encourage employees, and specify that there will be absolutely no repercussions, to discuss their reasons why strategic plan actions should be changed or eliminated. By providing employees with a safe environment for them to authentically share their input, creative suggestions, and solutions, you will begin to create an honest business culture that can lead to great collaboration, cooperation and success.

BEGIN AT THE BEGINNING TO ENGAGE EMPLOYEE BUY-IN

Assumptions are the foundation and a prerequisite to a great strategy. Executive management must use the most accurate data available to make assumptions about the business environment. These assumptions represent their opinions, beliefs and hopes *underlying their strategy*. Here is an example of an airline assumption: *We assume that fuel costs will increase by 5 percent over the next 12 months.*

Strategic projections are based on assumptions. Again, it is imperative that the data behind these assumptions be as accurate as possible. If the assumptions are unsupported, that could require changes to be made during the plan execution in order to still achieve the strategic goals, or worse, cancellation of the plan entirely.

Greg Githens, vice president at Strategic Initiatives and Innovation, states that, "Implementation teams have to accept the risks that assumptions might be wrong. Fortunately, following two common-sense rules helps avoid major mistakes: always document the assumptions in the plan and always validate them during execution."

"Developing and debating strategic assumptions with groups of employees is an excellent way to begin to get buy-in and commitment. With this buy-in comes a greater probability that the plan will actually be implemented."
—Mark Hollingsworth, President of 5i Strategic Affairs

You will also gain buy-in from department managers responsible for execution when you connect your strategic plans directly to their operational budgets.

ENGAGE, EDUCATE AND EMPOWER

In their book, *Execution: The Discipline of Getting Things Done*, published in 2002 by Crown Business, Larry Bossidy and Ram Charan talk about a specific set of behaviors and techniques that companies must master in order to have a competitive advantage. Execution must be thought of as a discipline and a practice that is essential to success.

Whether you are the CEO or line management, your goal is to create a culture based on execution and desired results. To create this culture you must engage, educate and empower those you manage to enable them to make informed decisions based on their knowledge of the company's strategic goals. Besides, employee engagement and satisfaction should be at the top of every company's strategic goals.

Execution should be reflected everywhere in the organization. As a supervisor or manager, it should be reflected in the department you manage. Execution must be part of everyone's actions, communications, meetings and reports. It should be practiced as an everyday discipline and is an essential part of strategy creation. In fact, good execution cannot exist without effective strategy, nor can effective strategy be created without knowing your department's ability to execute it.

To begin developing empowered employees and creating a culture of execution, you should engage your employees in the creation of strategic plans, goals and execution whenever possible. Frontline employees especially must be engaged in these discussions, as they will actually be executing the plan. If this is not practical, then invite one representative from every function who understands their departments' ability to execute. At the very least, you want a process that allows all the employees you are responsible for to have an opportunity to share their input. This empowers employees to automatically want to take responsibility and ownership for the strategic goals and execution plans they helped to create.

Execution is also the result of thousands of decisions made every day by all employees based on the information they have. Empowerment turns them into well–informed and capable employees, ready to effectively deal with decisions that, in many companies, flow up to executive management. They will be more proactive and creative in problem solving, which provides more effective decision-making and allows for a more smoothly run operation across all levels. An educated work force also helps a company seize market opportunities faster. Knowing that employees can make informed decisions, executive management can then fully devote their expertise to strategic and global issues and be better prepared to successfully maneuver the continually changing business landscape.

Being part of the creation of strategy/execution plans educates your employees in understanding the consequences of not achieving strategic goals. They begin to intimately understand exactly how their daily activities affect the success of the strategic goals, company success, their own promotions, 401 K's, bonuses and profit sharing. Employees who understand how their job function makes money for the company can also drive revenue growth.

TRANSLATING STRATEGIC GOALS INTO EXECUTABLE ACTION

To produce effective execution results, every employee must truly understand the strategy and its goals; therefore, state them as simply as possible.

An excellent visual tool you can use to easily communicate the strategy and goals to the entire organization is part of what's called a Corporate Level Strategy Map, created by Robert Kaplan and David P. Norton. You can use a Cascading Strategy Map to show how each department plans to support the strategic goals.

You can also use Strategy Maps to drive performance, because they provide a simple visual format for executing strategy. Plus, they provide clarity regarding roles and responsibilities relative to the strategic plan goals.

METRICS, MILESTONES AND INCENTIVES

Strategic execution must always include metrics and milestones that align with the strategic goals. Once employees understand the roles they will play in relation to the goals, allow them to give input to their managers to help establish their own goals as they relate to the metrics and milestones.

The first step here is breaking down the strategic goals that your department is specifically responsible for, into time-specific, definable, executable actions, metrics, and milestones necessary to progress toward those goals. Align these actions with day-to-day activities. This gives you a road map that will help you control the progress and address problems as they occur.

Successful execution also requires employees to have sufficient monetary incentive. Provide monetary incentives, positive feedback and praise for employees who take an active part in the execution of the strategic goals and successfully reach milestones. This communicates a strong message to all employees that execution is the new culture of the company.

ACCOUNTABILITY

There should also be absolute agreement between employees and management about exactly what the employee is accountable for as well as clarity in terms of expected time frames. After all, if an objective is not managed by time, it will never be completed or its progress ever evaluated. The smaller the number of goals assigned to employees, such as three or four, the better the chance for successful execution.

As an added benefit, management and employees creating and agreeing on definitive accountability aligns with job performance verification. Bring in the human resources department to revise and update job descriptions. Keeping job descriptions current is especially crucial, as they support the accountability aspect you need to maintain execution excellence.

When the execution plan is complete, make sure it is simple, specific and clear. What might look like resistance from some employees who may not have been directly involved in the strategy or execution, may be just a lack of clarity. The message should be very simple: these are the goals we are trying to reach and why, and this is how we will measure progress.

DIPPING YOUR STRATEGIC TOE IN THE WATER

Begin by engaging your department in a discussion that leads to a simple, shared departmental goal, and go from there. While the various suggestions I have offered will not guarantee strategic execution success, implementing them will greatly improve your odds.

When you, as the leader, can walk up to any employee you manage and that person can easily tell you the company strategy, the reason for that strategy, and how he or she contributes to the strategic goals and company success, you have begun your job as an authentic, and therefore effective, and successful leader.

Paula E. Pacheco
Pacheco Business Services
Educating Businesswomen to Successfully
Maneuver the Corporate Landscape
On Their Own Terms
408-966-5811
paula@paulapacheco.com
www.paulapacheco.com

Paula's passion is to help corporate women in management succeed in business by delivering high-performance leadership programs. She educates them on strategy creation and execution—a much sought after and difficult skill set that is highly prized in the business world. She also teaches women communication skills and how to maneuver the corporate landscape to successfully reach their desired goals.

Paula entered the corporate world at age 18. When she stepped into management at age 23, she proceeded to take the management and business courses available to her. This helped her become a dynamic, strong, results-oriented professional in operations development and change, who is experienced in analyzing, managing, training, growing and re-structuring business operations. She learned to successfully implement organizational objectives utilizing employee input, a team-building philosophy, supportive leadership, strategic analytical planning and business process methodologies.

Her diverse professional background includes Fortune 500 companies, including Bank of America, IBM, PGE, the Pacific Stock Exchange, the entertainment industry, the non-profit sector, high tech start-ups, the construction industry and West Valley College. In an effort to always provide her clients with the latest and best in business methodologies, Paula has been taking business courses at Stanford University since 2011.

Be Your Own
Soul Massage™ Guide

HONOR AUTHENTIC
PRESENCE AND EXPRESSION

By Vicki Takeuchi Wynne, MSW, LMT

*H*ave you ever felt there is more to your life than what is happening now? Do you ever feel anxiety, depression, or fear for no apparent reason? Is there anything you want to say or do in this lifetime before you leave? If so, I can help you.

I am a Soul Massage™ Guide. I assist you in finding the voice of your soul. Soul Massage honors and nurtures the total expression of who you are in this world. So much of life is external—the physical body, the everyday conversations, the job, the family. However, there is also an internal life which involves who you are emotionally, mentally and spiritually. I facilitate you going back into yourself and examining how you express what is true for you. I call this holistic approach Soul Massage, where the internal and external come together, balance and heal. You come back to your authentic self—secure, loving and open.

"When personality comes fully to serve the energy of the soul, that is authentic empowerment."
—Gary Zukav, American spiritual teacher and author

Soul Massage supports you when you want to be seen and heard, feel whole, healthy and at peace. Especially in times of transition and uncertainty, this approach helps you feel supported and comforted. When given care and attention with Soul Massage, you have a chance to awaken and become aware of how you choose to handle your journey of change, illness or life transition.

When you are in tune with your physical, mental, and emotional being, and can drop deeply into yourself—the fullness of your pain, your story, your healing—then you can truly express yourself authentically and can fully communicate your truth. Then, you are free to be yourself. That is my wish for you. What follows is how I learned to express myself more freely.

FIRST SIGNS OF ANXIETY

My father died in 1974, two weeks before my college graduation. Somehow I got through the graduation ceremony. I toured New York City with my mother and aunt, and then traveled to Hawaii. I had a full scholarship to the University of Hawaii, where I immersed myself in cross-cultural programs at the East West Center.

As a high achiever, I always felt in control of my life. I set goals and reached them. However, life had other plans for me. I began to wake up with anxiety, tension and fear. Even though I was in a beautiful academic environment, my emotions were flooding out. Every day I awoke in a panic, with tears streaming down my face and my heart racing. I received counseling and decided I could not continue my school program. I went home to live with my widowed mother.

ACKNOWLEDGING MY TRUTHS

I found myself taking a good look at what was going on in my life. As I went deeply into my own soul and listened, I finally gave a voice to what was real for me. I acknowledged my childhood trauma of sexual abuse, which I had never told anyone about. My body would no longer let me be in denial about a family member betraying me and breaking my heart.

Also, raging anger from a past relationship had taken a toll on me. Even though he was a kind, generous, loving man who would do anything for me, he had a frightening temper. I would be terrified and say nothing. I finally did start speaking up and suggested he get some help for his anger, which upset him even more. He did not believe he had a problem. He felt that he was just angry, a natural human emotion, and that I was too sensitive. Have you ever been told you were too sensitive when you became emotional about something?

You may wonder why I stayed in that relationship. As a young child, I grew up with a father who yelled a lot and a mother who said little. I did not say much either. Even though I was the first in my family to graduate from college and attain a good job, there was a part of me that had lost my own voice.

Have you ever felt as if you lost your soul when someone yelled at you? In my relationship, I eventually started speaking up, yet my body began showing negative symptoms. After some of his angry outbursts, I even went to the emergency room thinking I was having a heart attack. I was scared in the relationship, and I kept it to myself. I was waking up with feelings of anxiety, tension and fear, just like those I had experienced after my father died. I was also showing symptoms of post-traumatic stress disorder (PTSD), where I would jump and be easily startled whenever people came close to me.

DISCOVERING THE POWER OF VULNERABILITY

You may have areas in your life where you want to be more vulnerable and stand up for yourself. Through therapy, I became aware of how important this was for me. I needed to speak up to this man about things that were important to me. My physical symptoms were the result of not being vulnerable and fully expressing my truth. I was also enabling his behavior to continue in ways that frightened me. Being vulnerable opened up authentic communication for both of us to be more courageous and willing.

Together, we sought the help of a therapist. Having a third party to witness our journeys and offer guidance assisted our healing and understanding. We felt safe to express our true feelings. Therapy gave us a sacred space where we felt held and listened to.

We got massages, which relaxed our bodies and opened us to peaceful, nurturing, loving solutions and ways of living. We also took time to give each other loving touch/massage to connect on a visceral level beyond words.

Have you ever wanted things to change in a relationship, yet did not know how to make it happen? We learned different ways to be together. Even though we could not change the past, we were both willing to fully embrace the present. Being in the now gave us the opportunity to hold each precious present moment with all its possibilities and make choices that would create wonderful memories for our new future.

> *"If you are depressed, you live in the past. If you are anxious,*
> *you live in the future. But if you are at peace,*
> *you live in the present."*
> **—Lao Tzu, Chinese philosopher, author and poet**

Through my work as a Soul Massage Guide with others and with myself, I have discovered ways for you to affirm your authentic self and become your own Soul Massage Guide. I encourage you try these tools and see what they can do for you.

HOW TO BE YOUR OWN SOUL MASSAGE GUIDE

Three aspects of Soul Massage are Soul Touch, Soul Presence and Soul Expression.

1. Soul Touch is touch and massage that strokes the physical body, emotions, mind and spirit.

In his book *Loving Hands,* published by Knopf in 1976, Frederick Leboyer writes, "Being touched and caressed, massage is food for the infant. Deprived of this food, the name of which is love, babies would rather die. And they often do." Leboyer worked for years in India with mothers and their infants. He found that babies are nourished emotionally and physically through touch and stimulation by their mothers.

Touch is our first communication with the world. A baby feels safe in his mother's arms and knows the world is safe when he is there. Touch heals, nourishes and comforts in ways that words cannot. As adults, we continue to need touch. The stimulation and love that comes through touch helps us thrive.

Society's awareness has increased about how the mind and body affect one another. Your body holds many memories and life experiences within its cells. You even hold unconscious thought in your body about feeling tense or stressed, or how you move. Through massage, you can unlock and release emotions.

Some people do not receive love from their family. Some associate touch with pain or fear. Through sensitive and nurturing Soul Touch, massage can help heal some of these wounds of deprivation. After massage, you can feel your own sense of self and emotional calmness. You feel at home in your body. This is especially helpful to those who have experienced trauma and are used to leaving their bodies—taking themselves to another consciousness—to avoid feeling the pain and stress.

"The body never lies."
—Martha Graham, American dancer
and choreographer

It is also relatively easy to give yourself Soul Touch massage. Research shows that self-massage can lessen stress, depression and anxiety. It can also decrease pain associated with migraines, lower back stress and fibromyalgia, as well as reduce high blood pressure and stop cigarette cravings.

The benefits of Soul Massage come from the stimulation of pressure receptors in the brain. When these receptors are stimulated, the heart rate slows, serotonin is released, and there is a decrease in the stress hormone, cortisol. Soul Massage can also improve your hormonal balance and increase your immune functioning with diseases like cancer and HIV/AIDS.

Here are some Soul Massage techniques you can embrace:
• Massage yourself wherever you feel called to touch. Tight shoulders, stiff neck, lower back pain, and tired legs may beckon you. You can use lotion or aromatherapy oils to soothe yourself.
• Get a professional massage. Allow yourself to surrender into deep relaxation so your body can naturally integrate and heal itself.

• For couples, invite Soul Touch back into your relationship. Sometimes partners stop touching. When you begin touching again, your hormonal balance improves. Your relationship thrives again, like the baby touched and stimulated by his mother. You reconnect to spirit with Soul Touch.

2. Soul Presence is the embodiment of the divine, peace, harmony and acceptance.

In school, when the teacher calls roll and you hear your name, you say, "Here" or "Present." Most of the time you are just mindlessly waiting for your name to be called, and your response is half-hearted. You do not answer too loudly, to avoid others making fun of you. You do not want to stand out. You are present, but usually not *fully* present.

Soul Presence refers to a richer form of being present. Your presence on this earth holds all the positive qualities of your human spirit. What is your spirit telling you about who you are and what you want to become more of? What do you tell yourself? What pictures and visions do you hold?

What messages do you say to yourself? According to author Louise Hay, in her book entitled *You Can Heal Your Life,* published by Hay House in 1984, whenever there is physical, emotional or spiritual dis-ease, there are usually limiting thoughts and ideas that control and constrict us. We learn about ourselves and life by those around us. In her work with people, she found that for the majority of them their innermost belief is, "I'm not good enough."

Soul Presence is embracing the message of Namaste. Namaste is an Indian/Hindu greeting that acknowledges that the light in me recognizes the light in you. The deep, spiritual significance of

Namaste appreciates that the life force, the divinity, the self or the God in me is the same in all. I am enough and so are you.

> *"Feeling light within, I walk."*
> **—Navajo night chant**

HOW TO HONOR YOUR SOUL PRESENCE

- Practice mindfulness. Take a few minutes to become centered and fully aware of yourself in this moment. While sitting or standing, close your eyes and breathe in a fresh new universe of life. Exhale the old to release what you no longer need. Ground yourself in your body as you continue to gently breathe all the way to your belly. Plant your feet on the ground and visualize roots going deep into Mother Earth. Attune to your body—feet, legs, torso, arms, hands, neck and head—all filled with life energy. Breathe and affirm all that is in the moment. Be grateful.
- When life gets busy or you feel unbalanced, just stop—even in mid-sentence! Take a good, cleansing breath all the way to your belly. Breathe fresh life in. Release the old.
- If needed, be open to getting professional help. Many insurance plans offer benefits people rarely use. Get past any stigma you may have about asking for or receiving help. A good therapist or coach can be a helpful Soul Massage Guide to support your understanding of challenging situations and feelings. You can also set an intention of asking for help and see what people and opportunities show up for you.
- Respect your inner wisdom and voice. Trust your intuition, the gut feeling inside you that knows.

3. Soul Expression is authentic communication with or without words—exquisite listening.

*"Our lives begin to end the day we become silent
about things that matter."*
**—Rev. Martin Luther King, Jr., American civil rights activist
and minister**

As a baby, you felt free to express yourself. As you grew older and explored the world as a young toddler, you began to learn social norms from others. This shaped your expression in the world. You may have openly spoken out, made noise or shouted out, only to find someone telling you to be quiet, to be softer, or to not have a certain viewpoint. If you wanted to enjoy the peace and quiet of silence, someone may have told you to speak up and say something—something appropriate. Your confidence in expressing yourself became shaken. As a result, you may have become insecure about saying or not saying anything. Now you may be fearful of public speaking, or speaking in any situation. You may also feel self-conscious about what your own voice and inner wisdom wants to say.

Soul Expression means you can to tap into your own presence and feel held unconditionally to either speak or to remain silent. Whether or not you are speaking, you are always communicating, which is beyond words. You feel affirmed for who you are at the time, and you can speak naturally and eloquently without fear. You learn to honor the message that is meant to come through you at the time.

SOUL EXPRESSION GUIDELINES

- In silence, practice gently being with a partner's eyes.
- Be bold in your communication. Create beautiful venues and moments to have meaningful, important conversations with people.
- Learn to be an exquisite listener and hold a safe space for someone to be safely held and heard.

- Practice accepting others unconditionally.
- With a partner, take turns giving and receiving touch. Massage hands, feet and back. Do five minutes each. Increase time as desired.

Being your own Soul Massage Guide means that you totally accept yourself—your body, mind and spirit. Use these tools and develop your own that work for you. Get help if you need to.

The world needs your unique presence and expression. What is important to you now, and what message are you meant to give? Become your own Soul Massage Guide so that when you fully embrace the life you are meant to live, you feel the strength, courage, and freedom that inspire and honor the best of humanity.

Vicki Takeuchi Wynne, MSW, LMT
Be Your Own Soul Massage™ Guide:
Authentic Presence and Communication

510-703-9889
vwynne@comcast.net
www.vickiwynne.com

Vicki's early career as a clinical social worker focused on the inner world—feelings, thoughts and emotions. She expanded her work as a Speaking Circles® facilitator, helping people honor their authentic voice, learn exquisite listening skills, and develop ease with speaking. As a Certified Esalen® Massage Therapist, Vicki utilizes the quality of touch to heal, soothe and transform the body. Integrating all these skills led her to Soul Massage, through which she helps people feel whole and at home in their bodies, and feel purposeful and peaceful in their relationships, especially within themselves.

With a degree in psychology from Princeton University and a master's degree in social welfare from the University of California, Los Angeles, Vicki is dedicated to the uplifting of the human spirit. She shows you how to settle into your own authentic presence so that you can take charge of your life with confidence and joy, and become your own Soul Massage Guide.

Vicki participates as a director with Midori Kai, serving the Japanese and Asian-American community. She is also a music minister with the Inner Light Choir.

From No to Yes

DARE TO BE REAL

By Dot Claire, BSN, RN

How would my life have been different if I had known it was safe to be real, that I could speak my truth and would not be burned at the stake for loving myself and caring for my needs first?

Daring to be true to myself was radical thinking and not part of the feminine profile in the forties and fifties when I grew up. *The Donna Reed Show* and *Father Knows Best* were my models of family life and a woman's role. For me, the choices were marriage, teacher or nurse. Niceness and servitude were my models. In fact, martyrdom was a virtue. As a result, I found myself falling into the habit of saying yes, when I really meant no.

There were many times when I was afraid of displeasing others and did not want to look selfish. Therefore, I compromised myself for the sake of others. I think when I got married I said *yes* when I really meant *no*. Little by little, I lost my identity until the "I" in me no longer existed. I became invisible. My unconscious desire to be liked had become more important than being true to myself.

When I awakened from a deep sleep and opened my Pandora's Box, fear and anxiety met me head on. I challenged my role of the good little girl who obeyed family, culture and Catholic teachings from my childhood. In the seventies, I developed my courage muscle by saying *no* to birthing more children. At the time, I was overwhelmed raising six children. I questioned the sanity of adding more to my tribe just because the church said my duty was to procreate. Making that choice was my first act in caring for my body and my needs.

I spent years perfecting the "good wife" and "good mother" roles by numbing my inner pain with food. Humorist Erma Bombeck broke the Donna Reed myth of perfect wife and mother with her satire on motherhood. She kept me sane during difficult times. "Life is a bowl of cherries; it's the pits that are hard," she wrote.

At that time, I was stuck in far too many pits. My efforts at controlling everyone around me in order to look good began to fail. My emotional and physical health were at risk. I numbed my feelings by stuffing myself with food. My body reached a peak weight of 210 lbs. I hated the person I saw in the mirror each day. I had tried many diets, only to regain the weight I had lost. Diets clearly did not work for me.

AWAKENING

Feeling frustrated with my weight, I accepted a friend's invitation to an Overeaters Anonymous meeting. It was a God-in-skin moment. At my first meeting, I heard words of struggle and hope. Participants were real and vulnerable. I had come "home."

In working this 12-step program of recovery, the "I" in me found her voice.

I heard that I no longer needed to be perfect. Food was not the main problem, but a symptom of underlying issues. I discovered that reconnecting to the divine—God, goddess, the name you give for a power greater than yourself—was essential for lasting change.

> *"We all have a need to be visible, to be heard, to make sense*
> *of our lives, to wake up and grow and belong."*
> **—Anne Lamont, American author**
> **and spiritual teacher**

I faced a head-on collision between religiosity and spirituality. Surrender and forgiveness were the keys that lightened the load I had been carrying. I was responsible for my past misery, and I could change my story. I did not have to stay stuck and did have a choice. After being wedded to the drama of victimhood for forty years, this was a new concept.

Surrendering to the divine meant praying through fear every day. One of my sayings—I call them "Dot-isms"—is, *Courage is fear that is prayed about.* I was becoming a courageous woman.

Brene Brown, PhD, author of *Daring Greatly,* published by Gotham Books in September 2012, says, "To be authentic, to be real, we must cultivate the courage to be imperfect—and vulnerable. We have to believe that we are fundamentally worthy of love and acceptance, just as we are."

My search to discover and love the real me was under excavation. Similar to Julia Roberts' character in *Runaway Bride,* I had lost my identity by being nice and doing what other people liked. In the movie, Julia's character did not know how she liked her eggs cooked—fried, scrambled or sunny side up. She discovered she did not even like eggs.

Freedom from the prison I had created required tearing down and clearing out old beliefs that held me hostage from being a visible "light" in the world.

When I walked through fear and left a 25-year marriage, I said yes to me. I said yes when I left nursing and became a massage therapist. After the loss of my son in my early sixties, I listened to my inner nudge and left a thriving massage practice in Indiana to reinvent myself in California. Life is short, and I wanted to be surrounded by natural beauty and a creative environment where differences were supported. Daring to be real, to be truthful and resist the urge to accommodate my truth away was slowly becoming a daily practice. I was listening to my inner voice.

During my life, I have supported thousands of women through childbirth, healing addictive patterns, menopause—which I call "a pause from men" or "a time to discover me"—and completing the circle of life by midwifing them to the other side.

In my intuitive healing practice, I listen deeply. As I wake up, I hold sacred space for others to awaken, to be authentic, and to be at home within themselves. I love to create beauty and flow out of the ordinary. Today, my home is symbolic of my foundation. It is a reflection of who I am in this moment and who I am becoming. My home sings with happiness. Life is a blessing—even the pits—because everything has meaning and purpose.

I was inspired to use the acronym CREATIONS to build a foundation for loving and appreciating who I am. The following nine practices have guided me in identifying, shifting and stripping away the sabotaging patterns of my childhood, religion and culture. They helped me embrace, honor, and heal heartbreak when my son died.

They are the creative tools in my medicine bag that empower me to live an extraordinary, vibrant life in my mid-seventies.

C - **Create** a haven that loves and supports you
R - **Respect** your tears
E - **Embrace** fear with tenderness
A - be **Alone** without being lonely
T - **Treat** your body and soul with respect
I - **Initiate** laughter often
O - **OM** (a mantra consisting of the sound om) in silence
N - **Navigate** change with grace and ease
S - make **Sacred** ceremony and ritual a part of your life

Because the complete CREATIONS process is more extensive than space allows here, I will focus on three of these essential aspects. I hope they speak to you as powerfully as they resonate with me.

C ~ Create a Haven That Loves and Supports You

Move in *so* you can move on. Have you really moved into your home? That means you have unpacked those boxes, hung up your art, and finished home projects. Ideally, your home reflects who you are and who you are becoming, not who you have been. If you are not happy, your home will show it.

If you don't love it, get rid of it is my motto. Consider exploring your stuff and give it the *I love you* test. It may seem strange to start with "stuff," yet the truth is that clutter is not just an eyesore. It is a setup for confusion and overwhelm.

From my Feng Shui training, I discovered that everything has a vibration, even the pile of magazines and laundry in the corner of your bedroom. Our "stuff" either raises our vibration or drains it.

Whenever I am ready for change, I make it a practice to create a clear vision. I begin by clearing out my bedroom, closet, desk, or any area where "stuff" has accumulated. When a project is complete, I celebrate by sharing my success with a friend.

So unpack those boxes, hang up your clothes, toss items that are broken or you do not use. Get rid of old history that does not love you. Surround yourself with things that lift your spirits. A headline in Oprah's March 2013 magazine says it perfectly: "De-clutter your life and discover the incredible lightness of less."

Are you ready to put the timer on? Commit to 15 minutes a day for the next thirty days. Start now! You can do it.

T ~ Treat Your Body and Soul with Love and Respect

Did you know that your body is wiser than your mind and speaks the truth? It holds onto physical pain until you listen to it, say hello and attend to it.

I encourage you to love every inch of you—every cell, every organ, even the wrinkles and extra fat around your belly. Caring for your body is not something to do only in a crisis; it is something I encourage you to do as an ongoing spiritual practice. Do not be the busy woman who forgets her body until pain or dis-ease wakes her up. Without your health, you have nothing. Everything suffers: finances, relationships, travel and play.

Sit in a comfortable chair. Take three deep breaths in through your nose and exhale through your mouth. Now notice what areas of your body seem tense, tight or uncomfortable. Breathe into the pain and say hello. This exercise is about noticing where tightness and pain has lodged itself in your body. It is not about getting rid of it. Listen deeply to your body's message. Place your hands on the tight or sore area. Breathe in and hold your breath. Slowly exhale. Send love and kindness to your body through your hands. Notice what happens. Awareness is the key to change.

Here are some practices for alleviating stress and treating your body with loving care.

• Pause throughout the day, stretch and take three deep breaths
• Fill up your tank first before taking care of someone else's needs
• Take a walk in nature
• Soak in a bubble bath with lavender essential oil
• Massage your feet or get a massage
• Listen to uplifting music
• Call a friend and do something fun together

Explore creative solutions for treating your body with kindness.

S ~ Make Sacred Ceremony and Ritual a Part of Your Life

Author and visionary Carolyn Casey describes ritual as the means whereby we bring a story to life. *"If myth is breath, then ritual is the act of breathing…We connect with something larger than ourselves when we perform ritual."*

Simply put, ritual means "a repeated act." Sacred rituals create the space to focus on what is important to us. In ritual, you make commitments, forgive, show appreciation, honor community and reinforce beliefs. Every day, whether you realize it or not, you are doing rituals of some kind.

Rituals have guided me through many transitions. They have given me hope, a way to release the past and welcome new beginnings.

Ritual is in my bones. It is a part of everyday living, just like brushing my teeth in the morning.

When my 31-year-old son died, I learned to create beauty out of shock, anger, guilt and sadness. I journaled and cried. I dug in the earth while raging and crying. I created a magnificent garden honoring my son and cried. I hosted healing rituals and cried. Tears of sorrow were shed until I was done. I was just like Forest Gump, who ran until he was ready to stop. Mourning was a ritual that supported my grief. Women witnessed and held me through my transformation.

When two or more come together in ceremony with the intention of celebrating a transition, the energy or frequency of the group increases exponentially. Magic happens.

Sacred ceremony and ritual help you:
- Step into the present moment
- Create meaning out of your messy life
- Be grateful for your life
- Embrace change with more ease
- Take action
- Be at peace with what is

Transformation and magic happen when you implement the following three C's. These secret practices are key to your authentic journey to wholeness:

1. Clear and complete the past so you can be present to the moment.

2. Create clarity of vision or intention, so magic and miracles can naturally unfold.

3. Celebrate your successes with a friend or a community of wise women to witness, uplift and support change.

How can you shift from habitual rituals to conscious intentional practices that connect you with your inner wisdom? Do you have a ritual for staying positive or do you get stuck in negativity? Perhaps you are ready to start a new ritual that supports success.

Grab a journal or, better yet, decorate the cover of a composition notebook with stickers and your name. If you are an artist, create your own design. Choose one of the following for your new practice and stick with it for at least thirty days:

- Before going to sleep, write down what you are grateful for. Review the day and journal with the intention of releasing negative stories.
- Practice unstructured, unedited writing to reflect your observations of feelings. I call this "Stream of Consciousness Journaling."
- Record your dreams upon awakening—Dream Journaling.

Any of these practices will force you to stop what you are doing and pay attention to and listen to the sacred within yourself. Spiritual practices help you live the life you want by showing up authentically in the life you have.

If you find yourself stuck in an old story, repeating the same patterns, know that change is difficult to do alone. In my own life, when I released sixty pounds more than thirty years ago, I needed support from friends and mentors. If it had not been for mentors, friends, and a women's support group, grieving my son's death would have been impossible.

But change is possible. I now know that it is safe to be real. I can speak my truth and experience joy from loving myself and caring for my needs first and then enjoy serving others from a place of fullness. I know this can happen for you, too.

Leave what you have been to become what you can be. Spirit flows through you and through what you do in the world. Are you ready to be real?

Dot Claire, BSN, RN
Founder, Modern Day Medicine Woman

Ancient Wisdom for Your Vibrant Health

925-899-3746
dot@dotclaire.com
www.dotclaire.com

Dot Claire's medicine bag overflows. She weaves a tapestry that embodies vibrant health, empowering women over fifty to awaken their courage, activate their power, and create a joyful life.

Magically creating beauty and harmony out of the ordinary, Dot knows that your body and your living space are sacred TEMPLES that nourish the beauty of YOU. She brings nursing, healing touch, and aromatherapy to her work as a massage therapist and Reiki master teacher, helping you break through tension, stress and pain. As a Sacred Place practitioner, she creates healing experiences, ceremonies, and supportive sacred environments that help you enter into a deepened quiet place where transformation happens. Through speaking engagements, seminars, and private sessions, Dot passionately helps you raise your vibration so you can flourish in your life and business.

When Dot isn't exploring spiritual growth or being uplifted by a circle of powerful women, she enjoys nature, dancing, drumming and playing with her grandkids.

Contact Dot at dot@dotclaire.com for your complimentary Vibrant Woman Breakthrough Session. *She will empower you to dare to be real, live your truth, and become who you were meant to be—vibrant, whole and complete.*

Learning to Dream ... Again

ONE VISION AT A TIME

By Maria Antonieta Gomez, AAS, BA

The greatest success stories started with a dream. Those dreams came with challenges that either strengthened the dreamer's vision or changed their direction toward success. Quitting was not an option—those dreamers became "doers."

In my experience as a businesswoman with Ambit Energy®, a billion dollar retail energy provider in America, I have been surprised by how difficult it is for some people to dream. Some of them do not even believe they are capable of dreaming. People second-guess their dreams. Why?

Children have an innate capacity to dream. Some keep their dreams intact throughout life while others give up on them. Why do so few people make their dreams come true?

> *"Why stop dreaming when we wake up?"*
> **—Anonymous**

Just like when we were kids, we still have 24 hours a day to dream. Within those hours, you can also decide to make it happen, or you can sit on the sidelines and witness others dreaming. You can admire them as if dreaming were an exclusive privilege of the chosen ones, or you can take action to move closer to your goals.

Dreams vary from person to person. You may dream of having children, owning a luxury car, enjoying freedom of speech, having access to clean water, or living with rights we take for granted in developed countries. I have always dreamed of being a successful professional, mother, daughter and spouse. However, there is an irrefutable truth: the bigger the dream, the bigger the roadblocks.

> "A dream is an inspiring picture of the future that energizes
> your mind, will and emotions, empowering you
> to do everything you can to achieve it."
> —**John Maxwell, American author, speaker and pastor**

I have asked hundreds of people their secret to accomplishing what they set their mind to. Many had a burning desire to do what they felt they were called to do in life. They were patient, persistent, and enjoyed what they were doing. One of my favorite answers came from a successful young entrepreneur who said, "I created the opportunity that I couldn't find."

Successful people exist everywhere. You can find their stories in the wealthiest and the poorest countries, from Oprah Winfrey, "the Queen of All Media," to Malala Yousafzai, the youngest Nobel Peace Prize recipient in history; from Bill Gates, one of the wealthiest people on Earth, to Jay Z, one of the richest in the music industry, who came from the projects. Clearly, they were not all born and raised in the same circumstances.

Walt Disney lived during World War I and II. He was told at a young age that he was not creative enough to pursue his desires. Nevertheless, he managed to carry a big dream with him until he turned it into a magical place where both kids and adults dare to dream and smile—Disneyland®.

Why do we put our dreams aside? One common denominator is the fear of failure—the mass murderer of dreams and goals.

When I understood that the journey is part of the dream and is as important as the goal, I realized that it feels better to know you are one step closer. There is no guilt in paying the price for your dream like there is when giving up just because the journey looks scary.

I would like to show you, from the perspective of a young person who helps hundreds of people dream bigger, how much easier it is to dream when you keep it simple, defined, visualized and alive.

"All human beings are also dream beings.
Dreaming ties all mankind together."
—Jack Kerouac, American novelist and poet

FIND A COMPASS

Finding a close reference for who you want to be or what you want to achieve makes your dream more attainable. That does not mean you want to compare yourself to others. Every journey is different.

Mentors and accountability partners are your compasses. They are effective as long as you let them do their job. Like fitness trainers, they can tell you what to do, but that does not make things happen. To succeed, you must want the results for yourself more than anybody else.

My compasses are God and my parents. My dad, Edgar, grew up very poor. Going to a good school in Venezuela seemed like an unrealistic dream to him. He could not even afford a decent pair of pants, much less an accredited college in America. That was beyond his wildest dreams. He washed cars and polished shoes to pay for his school supplies. Years later, he graduated with excellent grades and won a scholarship in Venezuela. That took him all the way to Penn State, where he graduated as a metallurgic engineer. What could a kid with limited resources do when his family could not afford college? Only dream. His came with determination that led him to a plan.

Behind every successful project is a successful leader. Take your time to find that leader—someone you can look up to. If that person accomplished his or her goals, so can you.

DEFINE YOUR NORTH

Think of your goals as the north end of your map. You must define north to make your compass work. I encourage you to be specific about what you want to attain. Your answer cannot simply be "money," as everyone wants more money. Have detailed goals. Think about what you would do with that money. What would you change if you had it? Whom would you help? How and when?

If you are having a hard time defining what you want, ask yourself what makes *you* happy? What are you passionate about? You are the captain of your ship and responsible for your authentic life. It would be incongruent to only do what makes everyone else happy.

Dr. John Demartini, American author and founder of the Demartini Institute®, says that a lot of people want financial freedom yet less than three percent of them truly work for it. That tells me that although some dare to dream, only a few dream hard enough. Some want that financial freedom to meet the standards of the so-called American Dream, yet their intention is not genuine enough to make it a reality. Dreaming harder pushes you to the actions you need to take to make your dream come true.

Some unexpected obstacles may throw you off track. Life transitions, like relationship breakups or job layoffs, may have you wondering, *What do I do now?* Again, ask yourself what makes you happy. Your answer helps redefine your dream and creates a clear picture of where you want to go. That was my lifesaver when I came to the United States in 2008. I froze for a while, not knowing where to start. I felt overwhelmed by the language, the culture, the visa, the school, and the friends and family left behind. Still, I knew my ultimate goal was to be happy. *My* definition of happiness shaped my decisions.

> *"The two most important days in your life*
> *are the day you are born and the day you find out why."*
> **–Mark Twain, American author and humorist**

VISUALIZE YOURSELF SUCCEEDING

Visualization is the difference between your ethereal dream and the one with form and shape. *The Secret* by Rhonda Byrne, published in 2006 by Atria Books, reminds us that success is all in your mind.

To help your mind create success, I recommend making a vision board. Cover it with images of your ideal life. There is nothing more exciting than checking off something that was once a vision or goal because it has become a reality.

FOCUS ON WHAT YOU WANT

Gabby Douglas, of Virginia, was passionate about gymnastics, yet she could not afford to obtain the right training. She dreamed of being trained by Liang Chow, of Iowa, and declared him her trainer for the Olympics. With laser focus, she visualized it over and over again. Eventually, Gabby was able to train with him in Iowa while staying with another family, and she mastered her technique. She became the first African-American gymnast in Olympic history to become a champion in the individual all-around competition.

When you imagine losing, you lose. Why not see yourself winning? Try imagining the taste of victory after paying its price. See yourself receiving that diploma or earning that promotion. Visualize it. Congratulate yourself for making the effort to achieve your dream.

When potential clients ask me what happens if their dream does not work, I kindly suggest that they think instead about what will happen if it does work. Nothing makes your dream more powerful than a positive mindset.

If Gabby Douglas would have focused on her lack of resources when she discovered her passion for artistic gymnastics, America would have missed a memorable Olympics routine and a few gold medals that catapulted her to being a memorable gymnast.

"What if I fall? Oh, but my darling, what if you fly?"
—Erin Hanson, Australian writer

GET TO KNOW YOURSELF BETTER

Are you happier when you give up on your dreams to avoid failure or are you happier when you chase them at all costs? While it is great to know your strengths, it is also important to know your weaknesses. Here are some guidelines:

• Know your limits and delegate tasks. Let teamwork do its magic.

- Learn new skills. Allow yourself to stretch and grow.
- Do not let others steal your dream. If you are providing value and causing no harm, you do not need to defend yourself from unwanted criticism.
- Realize that only you can achieve your goals. When you lose yourself to others' doubts, you lose your battle. Knowing yourself means knowing your life's purpose.
- Keep your dream genuine. This keeps you strong when facing doubt and rejection.

"Do what you can, with what you have, where you are."
—Theodore Roosevelt, 26th President of the United States

CUT DISTRACTIONS

I knew very few people when I started my home-based business. When my mom told her friends about my new venture, most responded negatively and warned her to be careful about those "income opportunities." I did not let that distract me and kept going. A few months later, I replaced the income of a full-time job. I realized that external negativity was a price I had to pay for being out of the ordinary.

If something does not add value to you as a person or to your journey, do yourself a favor and get rid of it. Letting that heavy weight off your shoulders allows you to walk faster and attain your dreams more quickly.

Do not let the past distract you from the present. Sure, betrayal and painful experiences leave their scars, but when you learn to forgive and move on, you see the road ahead more clearly. I continue to work on this myself.

SURROUND YOURSELF WITH THE RIGHT PEOPLE

Studies show that surrounding yourself with successful people makes you more likely to succeed. However, the "right crowd" does not necessarily work with you to reach your dreams. Look for people who help you while respecting your goals and staying out of the way of you achieving them.

The people in your life are part of your winning team when they simply let you do what they know you are capable of doing. They believe in you, anticipate your success, and celebrate your accomplishments.

It took me a long time to learn to release people who had given up on their dreams. They distracted me from mine. Friends who started the same business with me and did not see results insisted it would not work for anybody. I kept going even when I felt like I failed them. Later, I understood that I am not responsible for anyone else's failure or success except my own. I learned this from the CMO of Ambit Energy, Chris Chambless. Had he focused on those who may not succeed, and therefore chosen not to start the company, he would have kept thousands of people from reaching their dreams.

> *"I'm a success today because I had a friend who believed in me and I didn't have the heart to let him down."*
> **—Abraham Lincoln, 16th President of the United States**

EMBRACE CHANGE AND FEAR

When I was younger, even in my wildest dreams, I did not expect to leave Venezuela; however, political unrest that started in 2002 forced me to leave the country in 2008 with my family and start over. I felt scared and lost as I began to redefine my life. I wondered, *Why me?* Then I began to see all the opportunities I had in front of me—opportunities that did not discriminate against anyone and were just waiting to be taken.

People think I had it all figured out. However, we all sometimes feel like winners and sometimes not. I invite you to see your challenges as the gym for your dreams, making them develop stronger, leaner muscles. Push yourself through difficulties and reach your potential. It feels great when you look back and see that you made it.

Feeling insecure sometimes does not mean you weren't meant to pursue your dreams. You have the ability to defeat the hurdles. My mother, Ana, overcame countless challenges due to her love for her kids. Your self-motivation determines the effectiveness of your compass.

> *"Man is a genius when he is dreaming."*
> **—Akira Kurosawa, Japanese filmmaker**

As a child, Akira Kurosawa endured World War I and the earthquake of 1923. As a lesson on facing his fears, Kurosawa's brother forced him to watch thousands of people die. Kurosawa grew stronger over the years and confronted the hiccups of his professional career. He directed his first film during World War II and became one of the most influential directors in the film industry.

GET IT DONE

When you decide to claim life's rewards, you do what you have to do. You can learn as you go. Yes, learning is important and defining your dreams is exciting, but you waste valuable time if you do not take action. Just get moving.

Arthur L. "Art" Williams Jr., founder of A.L. Williams & Associates, could not have said it better at the 1987 National Religious Broadcaster Convention. He said, "The key to winning in the United States is what is inside a person. It is your integrity." He mentions the importance of a person's abilities, character, commitment, passion and enthusiasm to do what they do. His mantra: "Do it and do it and do it until the job gets done."

BE THANKFUL

Once you have accomplished your dream, pause for gratitude. Then create a new, bigger dream. At age 29 I bought the car of my dreams, the one I had cut from a magazine and pasted on my vision board. After I left the luxury car dealership, I had to stop to wipe my tears of joy. It was the overwhelming feeling of gratitude, not the car itself, that caused my tears. I felt extremely thankful for finding a business opportunity that helped me quickly settle into my new country.

- If you reached one of your goals and are getting ready for your next step, join me in this ritual: Celebrate what you have—your health, your family, your business, your job. What you are now is a stepping-stone to whom you want to be.
- Stay humble and down-to-earth. Do not pretend to be someone you are not—the ego is not part of the dreaming formula. Staying "real" makes you more inspiring to people around you and also keeps you teachable and coachable for that next bigger step.

When you give yourself credit for what you have accomplished, you realize life makes more sense when you work for your own dreams. If you have not gotten there yet, I have good news: as long as you have air in your lungs, you still have time to do it!

Maria Antonieta Gomez, AAS, BA

Dream with your head in the clouds, your heart loaded with passion, and feet on the go until the job gets done!

504-756-2343
mag@yourmagdream.com
www.yourmagdream.com

Born in Venezuela, Maria Antonieta moved to the United States as an International Business Student. She chased the American Dream, became an independent consultant with Ambit Energy, and was financially independent within a year. As a businesswoman and speaker in the Hispanic community, Maria Antonieta believes the world needs more guidance in dreaming, owning the dream, and going after it responsibly. She received the Most Inspiring Woman award from the Ambit-ious Women Conference in 2012.

Maria Antonieta enjoys helping her family and friends, volunteering for charity organizations, and hosting TV shows in Houston, Texas. She is an actress and stood in for Sandra Bullock in the movie *Our Brand Is Crisis.*

Maria Antonieta has made it a personal goal to positively impact groups and individuals by sharing her story with thousands of people across the country through her organization. She expresses that overcoming her limitations is proof that when your dream is magnificent enough, nothing can get in the way. Helping others is Maria Antonieta's hallmark. She recognizes that only teamwork and a positive symbiosis make the difference between a dreamer and a doer.

Get Your
GLOW On!

By Katie Macks

M y intention in writing this chapter is to ignite your desire to invest in yourself and to do so with self-respect, compassion, kindness and GLOW— Growing, Loving, Opening and Willing. It is time to create the life you want and to allow yourself to take inspired action that is aligned with who you are and where you want to go.

What would happen if you invested in the most important relationship you have—the one you have with yourself? What would it mean to you if you could reignite your GLOW and live an authentic life? And what if you could be free of your "shoulds" and be able to make choices that are aligned with your values?

With the intense demands of our modern-day world, we often become derailed due to the multiple roles we play, from career mogul, to mother, to partner. It is no wonder that many of us face challenges in creating trusting and meaningful relationships with ourselves and others. We are moving at such a fast pace and are pulled in so many directions, it is surprising that our relationships function as well as they do. As we move through our daily lives, we are often influenced by our needs to be seen, to be heard, to belong, to be appreciated and to be acknowledged. As a result, we tend to do more and try to achieve more, hoping we will feel better about ourselves. This never-ending and distracting cycle has us focus on everything and everyone but ourselves.

Does this sound familiar? Do you find yourself operating out of a sense of duty and obligation to meet your daily demands? Are you finding that this leads to disappointment and resentment? You may feel victimized by your circumstances rather than responsible for the circumstances you have created.

At some point, you may be faced with challenges that offer you a wakeup call, like the loss of a loved one, a separation or divorce, loss of a job, a betrayal or a health crisis, and you find yourself asking, *How did I get here? How did this happen to me and what can I do?* If you are ready to take your life back into your own hands and focus on the most important relationship—the one you have with yourself—I can assure you that you will rediscover new levels of trust, intimacy, authenticity and freedom. You will reignite what was once important to you, but in order to accomplish this, you must be willing to put the oxygen mask on yourself first before putting it on anyone else.

YOUR PAST CONNECTS TO YOUR PRESENT

When you were born, connecting with others was a natural instinct. As you grew up, this natural instinct was overshadowed by events, circumstances and experiences that took place early in your life.

As Source Point Training© teaches in their Relationship Coaching workbook, published in 2010 by On the Mark Branding™, you made many decisions about who you were and who you were not as a result of your past experiences; yet when these events took place, you were too young to discern what was real and what was not. At some point in your early years, you unknowingly began to build a wall of protection around your authentic self.

For example, if a young child witnesses an out-of-control or abusive alcoholic parent, the child may feel at fault for the parent's drinking and behavior. In fact, the child has nothing to do with the choices the parent makes. She is not able to discern the reality of the situation and therefore may feel responsible for what is occurring. She may then take on behaviors to compensate for what she is experiencing.

Another example is a child who witnesses her parents having financial distress. She may assume that she is part of the problem and therefore begins to feel like she is a burden to the family. Like the previous example, the child is not able to discern what is actually occurring, so she may take on responsibilities that do not belong to her.

My own example is that I was put on my first diet at the age of four. My mother witnessed her mother gain and lose a lot of weight annually, which deeply affected her. She then unknowingly projected her fear of food and self-hatred regarding her body onto me. I interpreted this new restriction to mean I was not acceptable as I was, and there must be something wrong with me.

Perhaps you grew up in a stable and loving home environment, yet you experienced challenges at school or with other kids that affected how you saw yourself.

Source Point Training teaches that past experiences have a profound effect on how you view yourself and how you live and interact with everyone in your life today. Because of early life experiences, you developed beliefs, attitudes, assumptions, and behaviors about who you are. This creates patterns in the way you live your life and in how you create relationships.

> *"We don't see things the way they are, we see things the way we are."*
> **—The Talmud, a central text of Rabbinic Judaism**

The patterns you formed created a wall of protection around you to give you the sense that you are safe from being hurt. The irony is that our connections give our lives purpose and meaning, yet, when faced with the possibility of being hurt, rejected, judged, disappointed or abandoned, we unconsciously continue to add layers of protection around ourselves. These layers of protection divert us from our natural instincts to love, to be loved, and to belong. As we continue to add layers of protection around ourselves, we create and refine the image we strategically project to others.

You create your image so that you can reveal to the world only what you want others to see, and at the same time, you work hard to conceal parts of yourself for fear of not being loveable or acceptable. In this duality, you lose sight of your authentic, glowing self.

MY WAKE-UP CALL

A few years back, I found myself on an unanticipated journey. I was in uncharted territory. I felt terrified because I had lost touch with my hope, my passion, and my connection to myself. This profoundly affected my connection with others. In spite of how I was feeling, my image was intact, and I looked as though I had it all together and was living the dream. I had a very successful career as a real estate agent, I was going 24/7, and was at the top of my game professionally.

I received great recognition from my industry and colleagues, as I was in the top 3 percent in home sales nationally, and yet I rarely experienced fulfillment or joy in my achievements. I seldom felt I was enough—smart enough, thin enough, pretty enough or successful enough. As a result, I put pressure on myself to do more and accomplish more. My achievements were diminished by what I carried in my heart.

I felt a tremendous amount of shame and isolation because I knew I was disconnected from myself; yet I felt powerless to do anything about it. I kept myself so busy with clients and obligations that I had no time to think about how I could make changes in my life. I felt locked in, resigned and alone. I let my life's circumstances own me, and I became a victim to the very circumstances that I had created.

My relationships were suffering and I felt suffocated. The things I once valued seemed out of reach, such as spending quality time with my family and friends without distraction, cooking healthful meals, taking time for reflection, exercising and walking my dog in the hills. Other sources of enjoyment such as going to the movies or the theatre, or taking a true vacation without toting my work along, had all been forgotten. It seemed I just didn't have the time to integrate these essential nutrients into my life. As a result, my frustration grew, and I could not see any options for relief. I was stuck.

I also had big financial obligations, which conveniently justified the story I told myself; I would have to continue doing what I was doing or lose everything. All the while, I was getting older and wondered what else I could do for a career. Who would hire me in a competitive market? I was terrified to lose financial control and chose to endure and suffer. This kept me disconnected from my values, dreams and heart. I lost sight of future possibilities and let fear get the best of me.

THE PATH OF UNCERTAINTY LED
TO THE ROAD OF DISCOVERY

At the age of 51, I realized that there were too few years left to continue living without sustenance, without a deep connection to what was important to me, and without growth. Things began to change when I became willing to let go of my real estate career. The price I had to pay was to live in a state of uncertainty about how to transition to a new and fulfilling career.

I had no idea where I would land, but holding on to what was not working only stifled and distracted me from arriving at my new destination.

I was being called to something. However, with all the noise of daily life, I could not hear, see nor feel what that calling was. I realized my first step was to slow down and be still with myself without all the distractions. As I began to gain clarity, I decided to reach out to people from my past in the training and coaching profession.

Over the course of the next year, I connected with many training and coaching companies in pursuit of employment. One in particular stood out to me. We had shared a history, plus the curriculum and career opportunity they offered matched my vision. Unfortunately, after many meetings with the owner of this company, I did not think the income would be sufficient enough to make the change.

As a result, another frustrating year in real estate passed with no change in sight. Still undeterred, I decided to call the owner of the coaching company again. She challenged me to show up at her relationship coach certification training which was taking place three days later in another state. She let me know that she thought relationship coaching and training could very well be the doorway of opportunity I was seeking. At that moment, a quote came to mind from naturalist John Burroughs: "Leap and the net will appear." So I did, despite the fact that the financial components were still unclear and unresolved. I was filled with both excitement and anxiety for the possibilities that lay ahead.

I am thrilled to share that relationship coaching is indeed my calling. I discovered that the skill of building solid and meaningful relationships is the missing link in our growth, be it in our professional or personal lives.

My biggest awakening on this journey was coming to terms with the truth that I was accountable for all I had created. I had chosen to struggle and suffer, and to be the effect of my circumstances. That was a bitter pill to swallow; yet, simultaneously, it was the greatest gift that catapulted me to where I am today.

WHO BENEFITS FROM
RELATIONSHIP COACHING?

People often ask if relationship coaching is for couples. Actually, it is meant for individuals who are ready to invest first in their relationship with themselves. The relationship one has with oneself is the foundation for all other relationships in one's life.

Many of us are trying to make sense of how our lives have turned out. While we are busy trying to figure it out in our minds, we tend to forget to listen to our hearts. Many of my clients share that they yearn to become reengaged with their hearts. Years of habits and behaviors derived from patterns of self-protection have diverted them from their desired course. This, in turn, creates frustration and longing to be somewhere other than where they are.

Relationship coaching is about coming back home to your authentic self and reengaging with your heart and soul. You become awakened and conscious of behavioral patterns that no longer work for you. This awakening gives you the ability to create and choose new behaviors that are true to you and support you in getting you to where you want to go in your life. As a result, you regain freedom of choice and experience new levels of trust, intimacy, and meaning in your relationship with yourself and with others. Through this process, you reignite your GLOW.

GLOW: A PHILOSOPHY AND A WAY OF BEING

GLOW = Growing, Loving, Opening, Willing

GLOW is the essence that makes you who you are. When you are in alignment with your truth, your voice and your heart, you grow your GLOW.

Allow yourself to trust your GLOW. It lights the way as you traverse the many pathways that you take in your life. It shines light into your darkness and it illuminates what you may not be able to see with your naked eyes.

GLOW is your guiding light. We are always at choice to allow our GLOW to shine.

We are also at choice to dim our GLOW so that we may fit in or be accepted, so that we do not stand out or make waves. Are you holding back? Are you playing small? If so, you are denying your God-given gift to GLOW.

Were you told that you are too much, too emotional, too sensitive, too loud, too quiet or too strong. Maybe you have been told that you are not enough, not capable enough, not smart enough, not thin enough, just simply, not enough.

Living dim does not serve anyone. As a matter of fact, it diminishes why you are here. It diminishes your purpose, and it diminishes the most important relationship you will ever have—the relationship you have with yourself—which then affects every other relationship you have in the world.

It takes courage to stand in your GLOW and to be the beacon of light that you were born to be. As we allow ourselves the gift of owning our GLOW, we inspire others to step into their own GLOW. Your GLOW is authentic to you, and as we all let our GLOW shine, we have the capability to collectively bring to the world what is so desperately wanted and needed: connection, compassion and the vulnerability to take a stand for who we are and what matters in our lives.

Your willingness to GLOW has the power to transform all of humanity by causing a ripple effect of possibilities that are way beyond your wildest dreams.

What are you waiting for? Life does not happen to you, it happens *because of you.*

Katie Macks
Certified Relationship Coach
Founder and owner of Get Your Glow On, LLC

510-847-9757
katie@katiemacks.com
www.getyourglowon.us

Audiences intently listen when Katie Macks speaks. She quickly connects with people, holding them full of possibilities. Katie inspires new perspectives, incorporating heart and glow to show individuals that they can make the changes they desire in their lives. Katie believes that when people become aware of the attitudes, assumptions, and beliefs that drive their choices, they open up to possibilities they did not know they had.

With a degree in psychology, Katie worked as a leadership trainer for a San Francisco company. In her thirties she put her business career on hold to follow a dream. Katie embarked on a three-year solo journey around the world, primarily traveling to developing countries, and was graced by private meetings with Mother Theresa and the Dalai Lama of Mongolia.

Katie is a Certified Relationship Coach and the founder and owner of Get Your Glow On. She facilitates glow-shops, group trainings and works one-on-one. Her mission: *Get Your Glow On* engages and empowers growth-oriented individuals to live authentic and accountable lives, making conscious choices that are aligned with their truth and heart, thus creating a ripple effect of purposeful connection and meaning in the world.

Magical Moments

KEY PRACTICES TO WELCOME BLISS

INTO YOUR LIFE

By Patti Martin, PsyD

*A*s a 15-year-old girl working in a bakery shop, I delighted my customers by announcing their total bill, tax included. I did it off the top of my head—no cash register needed! I loved the looks I received. My boss loved it too. I was exceeding expectations and was a "good worker." I was also a "good student," "good daughter" and overall "good girl."

When I was 19, I recognized that I had a split within myself despite the positive esteem and accolades. I studied for A's, I washed dishes for my mother's praise, and I worked hard to please my boss. While the rewards of being a worker bee were seductive, I felt a little empty. I had a suspicion that the real honey lay beyond the varying forms of praise, paychecks and good grades. I found myself at a crossroads between my "pleaser" self and my "pleased" self. I was torn between the part of me who gave to get, and the part of me who just enjoyed. I wanted more of the latter. I wanted bliss.

Ahhh, bliss—fleeting, ephemeral, magical moments of uplifted joy. For me it happened in tiny inexplicable moments that invited my soul to expand. It showed up in the form of sunset walks at the beach while tiny birds danced back and forth in the sea foam lapping at the shore. It arrived when I read a line of poetry, listened to music, had a fabulous workout, or went for a refreshing swim. In these moments of vibrating and expanded connectedness, I would feel a unity with the universe that felt exhilarating, whole and happy. I experienced bliss.

These moments charged me spiritually as well. The banality of performing was edged out by clarity and oneness, flooding me with a love for everyone and everything.

I began to ponder how I could hold onto these moments of bliss. How could I expand them? The moments when I experienced bliss seemed random and far between. I did not always have an ecstatic experience when in nature or while listening to music. The answer was not just to slow down and stop being busy. In fact, when the busy work ceased—usually from exhaustion—I often felt disconnected and numb. In those moments of numbness, I would sometimes blindly seek the elixir of wholeness by turning to a lover, food or even alcohol. These were ultimately disappointing and poor substitutes for what I desired.

How do you align with the true sources of bliss? What are the keys to an authentic alignment that produce glorious, God-like filled moments? Wouldn't it be wonderful to feel at one with the universe and everyone around you at will? Wouldn't it be great to glide through your day buoyed by unselfconscious joy? Imagine having endless energy and clarity that allows you to powerfully manifest your life goals and intentions with deep, emotional connectedness and love. Oh Yeah! Where do I sign up?

*"Nothing is more important than reconnecting with your bliss.
Nothing is as rich. Nothing is more real."*
**—Deepak Chopra, Indian-born American author
and public speaker**

Most of our adult lives are spent out of alignment. From the moment we awake, life's unending demands and distractions throw us off center. We go through most days on a treadmill of thoughts and responsibilities that are filled with judgment, anxiety, shoulds, irritations, guilt and regrets. This results in stress, negative thoughts, frustrations and perceived obstacles that interfere with our ability to connect with life's bounty. Just as your car gives you clues that it is out of alignment by pulling to one side, we receive clues that we are out of alignment with ourselves when we feel overwhelmed, numb, stressed, fatigued, sad or lost.

In this chapter, I outline key practices to help you align authentically and discover how to connect with moments of bliss. However, this path is not for the faint of heart. We all yearn for simple answers, but experiencing the sublime does not work that way. Mastering the steps can be the easiest part. The harder challenge is surrendering and allowing space for the grace of the universe and the magic of life to deliver. You must learn the steps while also cultivating practices of opening up and surrendering.

Follow this guidance while also letting go and letting God (love) into your heart. I have created an acronym identifying the unifying theme behind these key practices to help you remember them. The acronym to connect with blissful alignment is **BE LOVE**.

BE A CHILD: LET GO AND PLAY

Children know bliss. Just watch them play. They express sheer delight and full belly giggles over silly, simple things. Think of how great it must feel to just laugh and delight this way—to make goofy faces, play hide and seek, run through a sprinkler, enjoy skipping with complete abandon or running just to run. Now watch adults. Our socialization tends to erase play except in a competitive sense. Play helps open up your core self and aid the connection and alignment with bliss.

Take a few moments each day to let go, be silly and play. You will feel more delighted and fulfilled and more closely aligned with your authentic self. This point is particularly important for women since grown men are frequently more in touch with their inner child. Most grown men love sophomoric humor, pranks, and getting down on the floor to wrestle with a dog or a child.

> *"It's never too late to have a happy childhood."*
> **—Berkeley Breathed, American cartoonist, children's book
> author/illustrator, director and screenwriter**

One day my three-year-old daughter casually commented that I was lazy. Immediately, the hair on the back of my neck stood on end, as I have never considered myself lazy. My husband, sensing my horror, asked my daughter for clarification. She noted that when we went to the pool or the river, I would sit in the boat or in the lounge chair, while Dad would dive into the water with her and her brother. My daughter was holding a mirror up to me and I realized that I did not like it. She was absolutely right. In my adulthood, I did not like getting cold or wet in the ocean, pool or river. Yet, when I was a teen, I lived in the ocean and was a member of the swim team. Nevertheless, my daughter only knew me as an adult, and she saw me as someone sitting on the sidelines of life, "lazy" and unwilling to have fun with the rest of the family.

That was an "aha" moment for me. I recognized how estranged I had become to my childhood world of play. I vowed to try to jump in the water metaphorically and literally whenever I could. Boy was I rewarded! Floating on my back in the river with my children, jumping the waves in the ocean with my family, or swimming while my girlfriends sat clothed and dry chatting poolside gave back tenfold. The initial discomfort of the cold water would always pass and be replaced by exhilaration.

Jump in the water. Find ways to be playful. Feel all your senses come alive!

ELIMINATE NEGATIVE THOUGHTS

Practice loving and affirming thoughts. The reality is that there is an inherent duality to life. The glass is both half full and half empty. Loved ones are dying and babies are being born. We choose where we focus our energy and thoughts.

> *"Perhaps all the dragons in our lives are princesses*
> *who are only waiting to see us act, just once, with beauty and*
> *courage. Perhaps everything that frightens us is, in its deepest essence,*
> *something helpless that wants our love."*
> **—Rainer Maria Rilke, Bohemian-Austrian poet and novelist**

Letting go of negative thoughts is easier said than done. You may not be aware of how pervasive and persistent your negative thoughts are. These dragons drain your energy, create anxiety, and fill your life with stresses and tensions that interfere with your blissful connection to the universe. Just as a car can hit a pothole and instantly become out of alignment, negative thoughts are potholes that derail you from your bliss.

Become conscious of your negative internal dialogue. Make efforts to let go of your negative thoughts and replace them with positive, affirming thoughts. Find a way to put your rose-colored glasses on and make dragons into princesses!

LET GO OF DOER-SHIP AND MAKE SPACE FOR GRACE

A large obstacle to blissful authentic connection is stress. Yet the stresses of our busy lives can be seductive. We feel important when we are busy and our lives feel full. When you ask people how they are, they often answer: *Crazy busy, there's so much to do.* Crazy busy does not open the door to authentic alignment and bliss. It opens the door to irritability and fatigue. Slow down, let go, and open yourself up to possibility. In surrendering and trusting, wonderful things can happen.

One of my favorite sayings is "Let go and let God." Life becomes magical and lovely when you understand that the universe supports you if you let it. Yes, you will still need to get things done. *Doer-ship,* however, is the feeling that if you do not do something, then an awful thing will happen. When you let go of doer-ship, you open up to the interconnectedness of the universe and the understanding that there is a larger divine intelligence involved. The path of bliss is one of self-effort and grace.

> *"The soul should always stand ajar,*
> *ready to welcome the ecstatic experience."*
> **—Emily Dickinson, American poet**

You have probably experienced synchronicity, uncanny coincidences or plain luck. These experiences tend to increase when you are intentionally engaged in your life and are open to other forces to support your intention. You can cultivate this openness by being aware that grace is like an energy system that is always there, ready to be the wind beneath your wings if you let it.

Many practices open your heart and soul to grace. You can meditate on a walk, in the shower, or on a run to help you let go of doer-ship. Even ten minutes a day helps. Contemplate, welcome and appreciate the divine in your life to help make space for grace to play a larger part in your experience and connect you to blissful moments.

OPEN UP TO THE MYSTERY AND MAGIC OF LIFE

See life through children's eyes. In their innocence and naiveté, in their unknowing, the world of young children is ripe with magic, mystery and enchantment. They are fascinated and thrilled with the most seemingly mundane things.

Reconnecting with your child-like wonder is another avenue to experiencing authentic bliss. As we age and pile on experiences, we become more jaded, more anxious, less believing. Try suspending your adult knowingness and experience the world as magical.

Most of us do not realize how dominant our unconscious thinking and our reactions are, and how these activities close in the walls of our consciousness.

> *"If your daily life seems poor, do not blame it;*
> *blame yourself, tell yourself that you are not poet enough*
> *to call forth its riches; for to the creator there is no poverty*
> *and no poor indifferent place."*
> **—Rainer Maria Rilke, Bohemian-Austrian poet and novelist**

In your busy life, awe, wonder, mystery and magic occupy dimensions you may not typically inhabit. However, if you remember to pull up a chair in their living room, you will be exponentially rewarded. Take a moment here and there to see something differently, to engage with someone differently—as though you had never had such an experience before—and do so with awe. Your first steaming hot mug of coffee in the morning, your child's sleepy-eyed *hello,* the moon rising in the sky. In doing so, the soul opens and makes space for ecstatic connection.

VALUE THE HERE AND NOW

Be present and increase mindfulness. Avoid spending too much time racing ahead in your mind to things you have to take care of. Do not ruminate over past experiences. These things fill you with stress—an obstacle that interferes with bliss.

"Oh dear, oh dear, I'm late,
I'm late for a very important date.
No time to say 'Hello/Goodbye,' I'm late, I'm late, I'm late!"
—White Rabbit, Alice in Wonderland

Practice mindfulness by attempting to be here now. Engage with one act at a time. For example, when you are eating, try to only eat. Drink in the color of your food. Delight in the flavors and the sensations of the textures. This helps still your over-busy mind and move you to the here and now.

EMBODY AND EMANATE LOVE

Connect with your feminine and be love. I used the acronym BE LOVE to help you remember the key practices for aligning, connecting, awakening, and discovering moments of ecstatic bliss. The final practice is to embody, embrace, exude, exercise and emanate love.

Quantum physicists tell us that everything is energy. The energy of love is the most powerful healing energy we have and it connects us to bliss. I am not referring here to romantic love, as that is just one small expression of love. I am talking about that expanding giving feeling of love that flows outward without expectation of return and connects you to others.

"All you need is love.
All you need is love.
All you need is love, love.
Love is all you need."
—The Beatles, English rock band

In your busy life, it may be a struggle to connect with feelings of love, particularly when you are agitated, stressed or depressed. It can be hard to let another car cut into your lane of traffic when you are late for work. It can be annoying when the girl at the checkout counter is more interested in talking to her friend than ringing up your order.

Feminine energy—in both men and women—cultivates a connection and relationship with your authentic higher self. Conscious effort to connect with your feminine energy makes space for the experience of divine love and blissful connection, even when just moments before, you were closed off and agitated.

To experience blissful connection, practice connecting with the following feminine states:
• Be compassionate, open and receptive.
• Nurture, share and be gentle.
• Exercise patience and connect with your intuition.
• Be empathic, warm, yielding and tender.
• Be understanding, responsive, helpful, cooperative, calm and creative.

You now have the key practices to welcome bliss into your life.

BE LOVE:
- **Be a child**
- **Eliminate negative thoughts and practice positive, affirming thoughts**
- **Let go of doer-ship and make space for grace**
- **Open up to the mystery and magic of life**
- **Value the here and now**
- **Emanate the love inherent in your femininity.**

Sublime moments of ecstatic bliss await you. The path to ecstatic, blissful, authentic alignment requires a focused commitment. As you actively work to replace negative habits with positive ones, you must also explore ways to let go, surrender and have faith. Move your focus away from the mundane rewards of being a "good busy bee." Open up to the divine. Engage in these practices for just a few minutes each day and you will begin to be rewarded tenfold. Namaste.

Patti Martin, PsyD
Feel better, Love better, Live better!

310-991-2632
drpatti@createyourchangenow.com
www.createyourchangenow.com

Since 2000, Dr. Patti Martin has specialized in helping women be happier in love by tapping into the power of their femininity and authenticity to improve dating and long-term relationships.

Working with humor and seasoned insights, Dr. Patti has an intense passion for educating women about how relationships work and how to stop the patterns that are keeping them stuck. She helps single women find the men of their dreams and re-energizes those already in relationships.

Dr. Patti offers workshops in addition to providing individual sessions via phone, Skype, or in person at her Los Angeles office. Dr. Patti is also a dynamic speaker and has several keynote talks that entertain, engage and teach your audience, including *The 3 Mistakes Women Make That Destroy Relationships and How to Avoid Them* and *Put a Ring on It! How to Stop Dating Toads and Find Your Prince*!

Dr. Patti Martin is a licensed clinical psychologist who works and resides in Los Angeles, California, with her two children and her husband and partner of 31 years.

Authentic Alignment with Your Feminine Resonance

EMPOWERED WOMEN IN HARMONY

WITH NATURE

By Shannon Murray, BS, BA, CMT

As a Western woman, you have a calling to make the world a better place. I invite you to embrace your power and be fully in tune with your natural state of being. You have a powerful voice and access to education, economic power and reproductive freedom. In your natural harmonic resonance, you harness your greatest potential to help the world.

At the Vancouver Peace Summit of 2009, His Holiness the 14th Dalai Lama Tenzin Gyutso stated, "Some people may call me a feminist... But we need more effort to promote basic human values—human compassion, human affection. And in that respect, females have more sensitivity for others' pain and suffering."

> *"The world will be saved by the Western woman."*
> **—His Holiness the 14th Dalai Lama Tenzin Gyutso**

You can become more empowered and more resourced than you ever dreamed of. I invite you to tap into the higher frequencies at which you naturally vibrate—your rich Feminine Resonance—to contribute to the world in extraordinary ways.

The first step is to understand your feminine body's inherent wisdom. The second and more empowering step is to live aligned with the cycles of nature and in resonance with its harmony—the true feminine power of this planet. Create the life you want as a balanced, vibrant, empowered woman. Achieve your life's mission and purpose in collaboration with the larger harmonic frequencies of nature.

UNDERSTANDING THE POWER OF NATURE

My background is in sound healing, acupressure and astrology. In 2011, I began swimming with the wild Hawaiian spinner dolphins. That was when my understanding of the power of nature became clearly evident. The dolphins were my missing link to living in harmony with my own natural feminine resonance—both as an individual and in community with others as part of a pod.

In my earlier years, I was wrought with self-doubt and low self-esteem. I turned to people-pleasing to ensure love. I felt undeserving. That pain has shaped me into the woman I am today. I now make each person I meet feel great about who they are. Everyone I encounter is an instant friend. I love this quality in myself and probably would not have it if I didn't know what pain is all about.

My life's purpose was ignited by the death of my older sister, Cathy, when she was 35. She was my only sibling. Her sudden death left a chasm in my heart because at the time of her passing we were not speaking to each other. I felt guilt, remorse and unforgiveness toward myself for more than ten years.

That experience sparked my spiritual journey and personal healing. It made me realize that life was really about loving each other unconditionally and freely. In nature, and with the unconditional, loving companionship of my dog, Solomon, my broken heart mended. I found sound, harmony and rhythm. Cathy and Solomon continue to bestow gifts upon me from above.

THE JOY OF EMBRACING FEMININE RESONANCE

I decided to learn about planetary tuning forks and Tibetan singing bowls. I practiced on myself. Unbeknownst to me, I was literally tuning myself up with the same vibrations found in nature and attuning my feminine frequency. The more I was outside in nature, the more I learned and the better I felt. It was the most natural body, mind and spirit experience. Like the proverbial pebble thrown into still water, the ripple effect keeps going and going.

My next voyage was to navigate my natal astrological birth chart. Understanding the archetypes, stories and mythology of the planets via the tuning forks gave me the background to understand the language of astrology. I discovered I wanted to help women embrace their missions.

I show my clients how to tap into their feminine rhythms, which helps them succeed in their businesses and personal lives. They embrace their true nature and align with their feminine resonance. They operate at a higher frequency and feel more accomplished and rejuvenated. They contribute more than ever to making the world a better place. They even still have time to rest, celebrate and take care of themselves. All of this helps set them apart from the rest.

HARMONIC TOOLS TO ALIGN WITH THE FEMININE

"When women awake, mountains move."
—Chinese proverb

Here are four tools to help you align with your Feminine Resonance:

- **Awareness.** The key to aligning yourself with the higher harmonic frequencies of nature is to understand and become aware of your true nature.
- **Access.** Easy-to-use tools for daily practice in aligning with your natural resonance are key to accessing the unlimited energetic resources available to you.
- **Acceleration.** Using your voice and consciously chanting ancient sacred sounds accelerates and harmonizes your frequencies.
- **Amplification.** Connecting with nature as you harmonize your body, mind, and spirit amplifies the resonance of both your inner and outer worlds.

Awareness. Did you know that you are a multi-dimensional being? You are able to exist at different frequencies simultaneously. Your body, mind, and spirit are each aspects of yourself vibrating at different levels of awareness, and therefore, on different vibrational frequencies. This makes it possible to be on multiple planes of reality at the same time.

Here is an example you may have experienced: You are driving your car. Your mind wanders to the grocery store or fantasizes about your next vacation in Hawaii. All of sudden you are home and you wonder how you got there so quickly. Simultaneously, you were existing in two or three states of awareness. Fascinating! Let me break it down for you.

The first level of existence is you in your body. The body vibrates at certain denser frequencies to keep you functioning and alive in the material plane of existence. Each organ goes through its functions and processes on its own. The inherent wisdom of the mitochondrial DNA provides instructions. You have to breathe, eat, drink, exercise, cleanse and rest. This is one dimension of awareness. It subtly operates in the background.

The second level of existence is your mind state. This is the area where thoughts and emotions vibrate as heightened frequencies. With ease, you can instantly accelerate into your future, relive experiences, create ideas, or transport yourself into another time and place. This can only happen at a faster frequency, in comparison to the more dense frequency of your body. Being able to transport yourself to the grocery store or swimming with dolphins in Hawaii while sitting in your car, driving 65 miles per hour, is amazing! This is a second dimension of awareness. It is more active and conscious.

The third level of existence is your spiritual state. This is the place within your heart where you feel higher frequency emotions like gratitude, love, joy, awe, forgiveness or compassion. You can send energy to loved ones, living or dead, or to special places. You can connect to the sacred. This frequency combines both body and mind, and is expressed through the expansive space within the sacred temple of your heart. This space knows no boundaries; it is timeless and infinite. This is a third dimension of awareness, more embodied and transcendent.

Access. Staying within the structure of body, mind and spirit, stop for a moment and tune into the three levels of awareness happening within you. Acknowledge your authenticity as a multi-dimensional being. Find a comfortable space where you can sit with your eyes closed. Breathe in and say hello to all parts of your beautiful, wise body. Explore its subtle frequencies. Discover where you feel ease and where you feel tightness. To the areas of tightness, breathe life-giving fresh air and allow your body to let go and become more relaxed. Your breath is one of your most powerful alignment tools.

As your body begins to relax, bring your awareness to your thoughts and emotions. Simply take note of what you have been thinking about or focusing on. Without judgement, observe what thoughts you find here. Are they repetitive thoughts on a particular issue? Are they focused on perceptions of what others are doing or not doing? Let your thoughts become clouds and watch them float away. Breathing in positive thoughts and mantras and exhaling negative thought patterns is key to allowing the mind to move from a beta brainwave pattern to a more mindful alpha to theta brainwave state.

As unproductive thought patterns shift and your body continues to relax even more, bring your awareness into your heart space. Move your hands into prayer position or place them over your heart. Feel the beat of your heart and acknowledge your beautiful ability to love. Relish this feeling of love. Think of something or someone you absolutely love, and focus on that feeling. Allow that gentle yet powerful frequency to grow and expand. Feel yourself lifting up from your heart, and open your arms to receive more. Tilt your head up and smile. Breathe in all the hearts that are alive at this time on planet Earth. Rejoice in the life-giving sun that shines upon everyone and everything every day. Allow your love to expand to take in every living being. This is authentically aligning to your most harmonic multi-dimensional self. You are amazing, beautiful and absolutely extraordinary!

As you become more aware of your authentic multi-dimensional nature, another powerful alignment tool you have access to is your own voice. You are your own inner tuning fork! The vibrations created by your vocal chords bounce off your bones, organs, tissues and blood, creating an echo chamber of resonance throughout your body. This sound is able to travel quickly within your body because you are mostly made of water—about seventy percent. Water is the ultimate transportation system for sound waves, which travel farther and faster in it. This is why you can hear humpback whales singing in the ocean from miles away!

Acceleration. One of the most sacred sounds we can chant is the primordial sound of the universe: *AUM.* According to Vedic philosophy, *AUM,* or *om,* is the primordial sound from which the whole universe was created. *AUM* is the cosmic vibration that connects you to the impersonal absolute, omnipotent *all that is.* The sacred sound of *AUM* also exists in the same three dimensions that you do, along with an added fourth dimension—material, mental/astral, spirit—and in the silence: the void of un-manifest creation.

Consciously chanting this sacred sound instantly harmonizes your entire being. You may be familiar with the chakras: the seven energy centers in the body through which energy flows. These energy vortexes are aligned, harmonized, and enlivened by the sacred sound of *AUM.* As you chant *AUM,* you balance your three dimensions and also receive the added benefit of aligning your seven chakras.

Here is an *AUM* exercise to accelerate harmonic alignment using your powerful voice. Find a comfortable seated position where your spine is lengthened and your chest is open. Take a few slow, deep breaths and come to center in your awareness of your body, mind and spirit.

Chant *aaaa,* as in the soft *a* in the word *mama.* Allow the sound of *aaaa* to continue sounding on your exhale. Open your jaw and allow the *aaaa* sound to draw your energy down into your lower three chakras: root (at the base of your spine), sacral (in your pelvic region below your belly button) and solar plexus (above your belly button). Continue sounding *aaaa* until you feel a slight buzzing feeling in your lower body. As this happens, you are harmonizing your lower three chakras. The sound of *aaaa* re-calibrates your being on the physical dimensional plane of reality. When you feel ready, begin chanting the next sound, *uuuu*, as in the soft u sound in the name *Uma*.

Bring your awareness to your head as you chant *uuuu*. This sound is much higher in frequency, and you are now connecting with your upper two chakras: throat (at the notch in your throat) and third eye (in between your eyebrows). Begin to feel this higher sound harmonize the center of your head in your pineal, pituitary and hypothalamus glands. Continue chanting *uuuu* until you begin to feel a slight buzzing feeling in your head. The sound of *uuuu* re-calibrates your being on the mental dimensional plane of reality. When you feel ready, move to the next sound of *mmmm,* as in the word yummy.

Bring your awareness to your heart as you chant *mmmm*. This sound balances the frequencies between your body and mind—that is why it feels yummy! As you chant, begin to feel that same buzzing feeling in your heart. You are actively harmonizing your heart chakra. The sound of *mmmm* re-calibrates your being on the spiritual dimensional plane of reality. When you feel ready, move on to chanting all three aspects, *aaaa, uuuu* and *mmmm* in one breath.

I like to do the full *AUM* chant by placing my hands in contact with my body below my belly button as I chant *aaaa* and move my hands up through the air to feel the space around my head as I chant *uuuu,* and finally move my hands to my heart as I chant *mmmm*. This movement of my hands helps me make contact with the corporeal and energetic spaces in my multi-dimensional self. Continue to practice chanting *AUM* in one breath until you have your rhythm down.

Finally, add the fourth dimension of silence to your chant. As you chant AUM on your exhale in one breath, breathe one full breath cycle (inhale and exhale) silently, focusing your awareness at the top of your head. This harmonizes your crown chakra. Silence after chanting AUM re-calibrates and brings all four dimensions— physical, mental, spiritual and the absolute— together. Continue chanting for five to ten minutes or as long as you like.

Amplification. Once you access awareness of your authentic, multi-dimensional nature and accelerate your alignment through AUM, there is more. You can amplify everything you are and resonate at your most vibrant state by connecting with other high vibrational beings and turning up your volume. Do this by spending time in nature. Nature contains the most resonant vibrations because everything is in its natural state of existence. Nature is dynamic and in constant movement and change, seeking ultimate harmony and balance.

In the forest, at the ocean and in the mountains, everything is alive and operating in its perfection. Spending time in such places reminds you of your own perfection—your own natural state of being. You receive Qi—life-force energy—from walking barefoot on the earth, sitting in the sun, feeling the wind on your face and listening to the ocean's waves rolling in and out.

In nature your three multi-dimensional states come into balance. The body rejuvenates, the mind relaxes and the spirit renews. Seek out a place in nature that speaks to you. Practice your awareness and chant the sacred sound of *AUM*. See what begins to shift around you as you come into more harmonic alignment with your authentic feminine self.

MOVE FORWARD TOWARD AUTHENTIC ALIGNMENT

Now you can acknowledge the unlimited source of power within you. Write down what most interested and resonated with you. Next, list three action steps to living more in alignment with your natural feminine vibration. Here's to saving the world with one harmonic woman at a time! *Aaauuummmm.*

Shannon Murray, BS, BA, CMT
Speaker, Author, Educator, Mentor
Shen Sounds, Inc.

AUM is where the heart is.
510-846-2148
shannon@shensounds.com
www.shensounds.com

Shannon Murray believes women are designed to be authentic as empowered entrepreneurs and leaders when they align with the powerful cycles of nature. Throughout her twenty years working in the environmental field, Shannon realized the key to successful environmental sustainability is rooted in a spiritual connection to nature. Shannon has discovered her pioneering philosophy; the power of sound is a universal language that awakens you to your inherent, natural vibration as a complex, multi-dimensional being who is connected to all living species. She is a leader in environmental stewardship and the divine reawakening of the feminine.

In 2007, Shannon launched SHEN Sounds, Inc., to awaken, develop and empower spirituality. She is a trusted companion and teacher who opens the door of the mind to walk the path of the heart. Shannon takes people from ordinary to extraordinary as she bridges science and spirit, simplifying complex theories with wisdom, storytelling and humor.

Download Shannon's free *3 easy ABCs for Instant Harmony* from her website: www.shensounds.com. Sign up for her course, *Lunar Living: Aligning with the Feminine,* at a special price with the code: FEM20. Join her Facebook community and connect with other like-minded, like-hearted, awesome women.

Don't Lose Heart in Tribulation

FOR IT'S YOUR GLORY

By Kecia Hayslett, RN

I awaken out of my sleep with a frightening vision of myself lying in darkness, in a bed of regret, sadness and rage. As I lie there frozen in that moment, a 17-year-old high school girl, tears the size of rain drops were running down my face, filling the pillow with wetness.

There I was, a senior, preparing for graduation and my future, envisioning myself as a college student. Attending college would allow me to have an opportunity to make better choices in life. I would learn to see life through a different pair of glasses.

As I was getting ready for school that morning, I noticed I was not feeling my best. It felt as if my insides had been repositioned to another part of my body. I continued to get dressed for school, as if it were a normal day. I looked in the mirror as I brushed my teeth, thinking and hoping that this discomfort was not what I thought it was.

Walking to school was enjoyable. I engaged in conversation with my girlfriends, laughing as if there were not a care in the world. One of the girls in our group interrupted the conversation and asked, "What if you have done something you know you shouldn't have done? Does that mean you don't get another chance to be aligned with your path in life?" There was silence as we all looked at each other in confusion. You should have seen the looks on our faces, especially mine, because in that moment I thought she knew what I had experienced earlier that morning. No one answered the question. We just kept walking to the schoolhouse.

As I approached the school building and walked up the first flight of stairs, I felt that repositioned feeling again. This time I wanted to bring out of me whatever it was that was causing so much havoc. Not able to verbalize this information to anyone, I grabbed my personal items and went running down the school hallway. I heard the stern voice of Mrs. Johnson, who was shouting from the classroom doorway, "Hey, Kecia! You know there is no running in the hallways. Walk! And if I have to remind you again I will have to take you to the principal's office." I was not controlled by her threat and continued to sprint to the bathroom.

A stall was the only place where I could have a moment by myself. *Oh my,* I said to myself, shaking. I can't be pregnant. I vomited, hoping no one would come in and find me out, and fled the ladies room.

I walked anxiously to the school office and requested to be excused from school. The guidance counselor told me she would have to call my parents. I shouted that it would not be necessary and that I could wait until school was over. It felt like an eternity.

I convinced my mom to make me an appointment to get a physical for school. On the way to the appointment, my knees were knocking. Sweat beaded on my forehead and my body shook.

The doctor confirmed the very thing I did not want to hear. "Kecia, you are four weeks pregnant." I told her that I thought she might have picked up someone else's results. She assured me that the results were mine. I screamed, "My life is over! There is no college for me! My mom is going to hate me and be very disappointed in me."

At home, I confided in my sister, Andrea, who promised she would not share my secret with my mother or anybody else until I was ready. Two days later, however, she had done something wrong and was going to get a spanking. When my mom raised the belt to spank her, she shouted, "Mom, Kecia is pregnant!" The spanking was given to me instead.

With disappointment in her eyes, my mom said, "Kecia, what have you done?"

> " 'For I know the plans I have for you,' declares the Lord, '
> plans to prosper you and not to harm you,
> plans to give you hope and a future.' "
> **—Jeremiah 29:11 (NIV)**

I went on to have my beautiful baby girl and adjusted to my new lifestyle as a teenage mother. Thanks to my mother—the greatest supporter in my life—I was able to do what I promised myself: finish high school. My mother quit her job to babysit Erica. I remember telling myself that I would finish and graduate with the same classmates I started with.

After high school, I decided to leave my home in Chicago, Illinois. I knew that if I did not change my surroundings, my surroundings would eventually change me. I was not going to let that happen. I moved more than 500 miles away to Minneapolis, Minnesota. I needed to secure a better future for my daughter and me. I needed to find a way for us to have a safe place to live and food to eat. At that time, I only had one child. That was more than enough, especially since I had no money, job or higher education to support my family.

There was a dance contest going on at the local lounge. The prize was $500. I entered the contest, took on the challenge, and won the $500. That was enough money to purchase a car, and buy gas and a sandwich for my daughter and me.

I was accepted at Minneapolis Technical College to pursue my License Practical Nurse (LPN) certification. Once I earned my certification, I was accepted into St. Catherine University and studied nursing. I graduated and became a registered nurse.

With the help of my church family, I was able to support Erica through high school, and she graduated.

If you do not like whatever is showing up in your life today, you have the power and authority to change it and create the world you want. I said my life was over, yet it had only just begun. I am grateful that God had a different plan for me. He has a different plan for you too.

If you are in a difficult life transition and do not think you can handle it, I assure you that you can. Every fragment of your life will be used and offered as a sweet fragrance unto God.

SIX STEPS TO AUTHENTIC ALIGNMENT

Six strategies were key to helping me realign my life. With these, I was able to complete college as a single mother and embrace my glory. I encourage you to take action with these steps if you are ready to move forward and find joy in your life.

1. Decide. Make the decision to shine in your glory. A confused mind does nothing. The Latin root word for *decide* means to cut down or cut away. Therefore, to make a decision is to cut away all other unfruitful possibilities and make your success nonnegotiable. It is only when you dig your heels in the dirt that what you want begins to show up.

Decide if your failure or setback needs a period or a comma. A period means *full stop—end of story*. A comma means *pause, transition or hold on*. Decide on whatever you want and believe it is possible for you. Declare it. Believe it. Act as if it were true.

2. Forgive. Forgiveness is a powerful quality to possess. Without it, you are unable to move forward. Get rid of old bags of hate, bitterness, regret, shame, rage and woe-is-me attitude. If you are trying to get through a new door of happiness, joy and bliss, I assure you that those extra bags you have been carrying around for years will not fit through the new door. If you are not sure how to forgive after you have been wronged or hurt, a great place to start is to ask God for help. With knees knocking and teeth grinding, embrace the new you that you are becoming. Forgive yourself, bless your past, and walk in confidence into your future.

3. Write it down. Write down your vision and goals as if anything were possible. It becomes the picture that creates the passion. Thoughts alone can be lost in the noise of life. Writing things down gives them substance and serves as a reminder. To see your vision is to call what's inside of you, out. An example would be the birthing of a baby. The baby is carried for approximately 40 weeks and the parents are envisioning what the baby will look like. They cannot see actual features so the features have to be in a vision, calling what's inside, out. You have to be relentless and tenacious to keep your vision alive. A vision without action is an illusion.

4. Get leverage. Go where you can learn a new skill or enhance those you already have. Consider taking a class. Join a networking or business group. Where can you find your tribe? Your community of like-minded people? Do you need an accountability program to remind you of what you said you wanted to do in life? I believe you must align yourself with the right people, places and things. Please know that you do not have to grow alone. There was a time in my life when I did not ask for nor seek any help because I thought I had to be Superwoman. Well let me tell you, it felt really good to take off the red, white and blue cap. Today I am not afraid to ask for assistance and raise my hand when I need to. My muscle of courage is strengthened each time I take the opportunity to connect myself to someone who is ten steps or so ahead of me. Then all I have to do is hook my caboose onto their train, with their permission, and learn all that I need to learn and grow so that I'll be in a position to serve for someone else in the same way.

5. Have a positive mindset. Continue to remind yourself of who you are and who you are becoming. What does it take for you to push past your limiting believes and stand in your greatness? Alone with the positive mindset, I had to stop seeing myself as a floating extension cord of possibilities and potential. I had to ground myself into a power source greater than myself, and I chose to plug into Jesus Christ. The truth is, Jesus did not just teach faith, He told us to have faith. Create meaningful affirmations and repeat them to yourself out loud throughout the day. Examples are: *I am worthy. I am loved. I have unlimited possibilities. I am manifesting abundance in my life.*

6. Feel gratitude and practice praise. I believe you get what you give. There is a universal law that has been put into place to help cushion the blows of life, and that law is found in Galatians 6:7 KJV: "Be not deceived; God is not mocked: for whatsoever a man soweth, that shall he also reap." When you sow seeds of gratitude and praise, that will be your harvest.

Be aware of your position relative to others. Focus on what is good, and make good grow—that is gratitude. Although life is not perfect and has trials and tribulations, life is good. Being grateful allows you to focus on the truth that you are wired for love, power and a sound mind. Be grateful for who you are right now, as you are perfect in every way. Be grateful for others. Take the time to look others in the eyes and say *I appreciate you for your kind words and support.*

Do not let tragedy be the only reason you think about gratitude and praise. Be thankful for everything—the air you breath, the water you drink and the freedom to choose. Decide whether to go outside and stand in the sun or not. Gratitude is one of my favorite steps in my journey to alignment with myself and others.

I want you to believe in yourself and love who you are created to be. You are not a mistake or an accident; you are predestined for an assignment. Find out what that assignment is and get busy growing and building.

> *"Beloved, I wish above all things that thou*
> *mayest prosper and be in health, even as thy soul prosper."*
> **—3 John 1:2 (KJV)**

Believe in the power that you stand in and know that there is no real doing in the world without first *being*. You are not a mistake and God has a plan for your life. Connecting with yourself and the one who is greater than you allows for growth. It is impossible to cling to what is comfortable and step into the next best and greatest version of yourself at the same time. Your net worth will never exceed your self-worth. I encourage you to take the six steps to authentic alignment so that you can reach your true potential and enhance your life.

Kecia Hayslett, RN
Hayslett Enterprise, LLC

Be bold, be courageous, be you!

612-408-3433
khayslett@gmail.com
www.keciahayslett.com

Kecia Hayslett is the CEO of Hayslett Enterprise, LLC, offering the Take It Head On Institute. Her mission is to help women embrace their star within and achieve personal greatness through balance in work and life. She is known as a provocative-thought leader and personal growth teacher. Kecia prides herself on teaching women to stand in their personal power and transition from an unfulfilled relationship to a place of self-love and self-worth.

Kecia overcame the challenges of teenage motherhood and living on welfare. Through perseverance, she graduated high school and went on to earn her Licensed Practical Nurse certification at Minneapolis Technical College. Kecia then studied nursing at St. Catherine University, where she became a registered nurse.

Today, Kecia is a noted speaker, author and life coach. She inspires women to stop waiting to exhale and to breathe right now! Kecia is known for delivering her message with compassion, humor and truth. Her greatest pleasure is to serve from a place of authenticity and authentic love.

The Art of Looking
in the Other Direction

By Carla Carroll, NMLS, CA BRE

I was born in San Francisco, California, and grew up throughout the Bay Area. I love the progressiveness of California. It seems that so many things started here. As a little girl, I watched elements of the Civil Rights Movement and the hippie era from a front row seat.

My father was a conservative-looking businessman with liberal views. On Saturdays, he frequently took me and my two younger sisters to a big park in Berkeley to listen to bands play and watch hippies. They mingled and danced with the spirited freedom of birds, yet were grounded on earth to propel change. I think he secretly yearned to embrace their spirit and relinquish his uptight lifestyle for a more peaceful and compassionate existence. He did have a more relaxed lifestyle at a later period in his life.

After high school I ventured to San Jose, where I attended San Jose State University. I started my career at IBM® and then worked for Hewlett-Packard.®

California provided me with the opportunity to be on the cusp of change involving the high-tech computer revolution. I worked in a world of brilliance and some eccentricity. I worked a lot. The perks were sometimes astonishing. My husband and I have travelled the world for business and pleasure. I am extremely grateful.

I have always loved and embraced adventure. After 14 years at Hewlett-Packard, restlessness brought me to several "dot-com" companies and two initial public offering events.

My parents and grandparents were originally from Louisiana. I am grateful that my parents gave me a spiritual background and showed me grace and manners. I appreciate that, as African-Americans, they did not teach me racism and never gave me a reason to feel inferior. At the same time, I watched and admired my parents' activism in racial and social issues at my school and in the community. My father was also active in behind-the-scenes politics. There was opposition to "busing" intercity youths in. My mother helped champion the cause for a higher quality education.

Unfortunately, after twenty years of marriage, my parents divorced. I was in high school at the time, and this was, perhaps, my first startling life change. My mother was struggling emotionally and financially, so I began to learn how to cope independently. Who do you ask for help when you are a teenager? I did not know.

Later in life, I met and married my husband, and we had a son. With a baby in our lives, it no longer seemed to make sense for both of us to continue enduring a grueling daily commute. Therefore, I chose a job in the mortgage industry as a way to work closer to home. This allowed me to embrace being a mother to the joyful son who had been bestowed on my beloved husband and me. My husband continued to work in Silicon Valley.

After I started working in town, I wanted to learn more about my community and find ways to contribute to it. I decided to volunteer for a non-profit organization where I was invited to become a board member. A fascinating adventure began. I met many bright people with huge, caring hearts. I learned about families in the community who had donated money, time and gifts to the organization. I learned about fundraising, board protocol, running programs, and the needs of many families in the community. I had previously been unaware of some of the harsh realities in the area.

My high-tech background brought something different and energetic to the board. Over time I felt valued. I was happily working and also serving the community. I loved the board and its members. I attended local and national conferences where I gained new skills and knowledge. The more I gave, the more I got back. While I worked hard, I laughed, smiled, stretched my capabilities and felt my heart expand. Then, things changed.

WHEN ONE DOOR SLAMS CLOSED

I was on the board for seven years. For a year, I had been feeling pangs in my stomach that I was ready to go. The thrill, passion and joy of doing the work had dissipated. However, I had brought a friend onto the board who had done so well that she was asked to be the next president. I did not feel right leaving her while she was learning to take the reins. As a past-president, I could offer her support and guidance. Plus, I just felt that I should be "present."

Then, a series of events occurred that were startling. They caused me to see some people and things in a different light. Some situations had not been handled well. A young staff member handled a situation involving a child in a way that I did not agree with. I knew the child who disclosed the mishandling to me. The staff member was eventually terminated.

During the investigation, some board members wanted the situation swept under the rug. I witnessed support for those who had significant funds to donate. I was shocked by the ethics displayed. Differences of opinions will happen in organizations; however, I found this one extremely disturbing. I was startled, unhappy, and mistreated as well. I realized I did not need that in my life. I was a busy, working woman who was also donating her time. I was done.

I resigned, as did the current president and my friend, the president-elect. We felt blindsided. I felt a sense of loss. I would miss the regular encounters, relationships, meetings and meaningful work. There was a void. The three of us started to meet for lunch monthly to commiserate. Out of this, a special friendship grew. In different ways, we all moved forward in our lives. Our purposes shifted.

Eventually, I no longer felt the pangs or even nostalgia. I continue to get together regularly with some of the great people from the organization. I highly value my experience with the organization, and overall it was a wonderful episode in my life.

My cousin later gave me the insight that seven years is a spiritual cycle. (I left Hewlett-Packard after 14 years—two cycles of seven years.) That makes so much sense. I have come to realize that deep and meaningful life-changing experiences are supposed to end. Challenges occur throughout life. A long-term relationship suddenly ends. Someone close to you moves away or dies. You change jobs. You move to a new location. You change direction or focus. Someone hurts or disappoints you deeply. The occurrences can be extremely painful. However, I believe these shifts have a purpose that is ultimately for your good.

Forgiveness plays a big part in moving to the next cycle of life. You must forgive those who hurt or disappointed you. You must also forgive yourself. This does not mean that you should not re-evaluate people and situations. You must learn from the experience and move forward.

PAIN STRENGTHENS YOU

Some life transitions come with searing pain. You may lose sleep, feel deep loss and isolation, experience emotional upheaval or suffer sadness. These are transitory emotions. You may question relation-ships during times like these. You make decisions to eliminate some relationships and to keep others. At the other end is a deep strength you never experienced before.

You may feel out of your element, adrift, or question whom to trust. You may be unsure of your own thoughts and feelings. Take solace in the support of friends and family you can count on. Consider turning to church or spiritual endeavors. Reading, prayer, meditation or journaling may give you comfort. Some people seek counseling. Feel free to cleanse through tears. Vulnerability is part of the process.

THE NEW DOORPLATE

It is amazing when you realize there is a new door to walk through. I have experienced this multiple times. Once I left the non-profit organization, it took less time than I thought before I no longer missed it. I began spending my time on the important and compelling things I was supposed to be focusing on. I felt a freedom to shift my efforts and energy.

WALKING THROUGH THE DOOR

You must boldly walk through the new door. You will encounter new challenges and also exciting adventures and opportunities for growth. Yes, you can expect melancholy when there is change. You are not the same person you were before taking that leap. Look forward to the new, key people who will be waiting for you. These people will emerge to help you with your new goals and life's purpose. They are part of your next chapter.

MY BREAKTHROUGH

Pushing through and enduring life's challenges can lead to break-throughs. Realize that the past is over. The sky clears and you can release negative feelings. You may even feel exhilarated. The future looks like a great place. You become excited about setting new goals. Find inspiration from people who show up with great stories to tell and gifts of new information to share. Recognize and embrace these remarkable people. They match the new level you aspire to.

A lady I met in one of my networking groups has emerged in my new life chapter. We chatted briefly during networking events, and she initiated a meeting with me. There, we discussed our mutual businesses and got to know each other. Since then, I have seen her give presentations. She shares experiences and recommends books. In one presentation, she shared that she had gone through a difficult period in her life and told the group about *Simple Abundance,* a book that helped her emerge from her dark period. Her vulnerability made attendees embrace her. I decided to read the book and have shared it with others. She and I spent a weekend at a business conference together, where we talked, laughed, shared and learned. My new friend has incredible energy and light.

FEELING FREER AND LIGHTER

When you let go of baggage—which may be a person, an organization, your work, or some other negative entity—you feel freer and lighter. The process of letting go is also a benefit of maturing. Pain forces you to focus, and the important things in life crystalize. You learn to spend less time on silly or time-wasting activities. You can spend time on work, not worrying about needless political or dramatic office trivialities. You spend your play time with whom you want, and you can engage in endeavors that replenish your soul and give you joy. You can even do nothing at all and just be quiet with yourself. I love the simplicity of sharing a snack or meal with my husband or son.

Sometimes after seemingly bad or weird things happen, my husband and I sit at the breakfast nook laughing and laughing. Instead of obsessing over the strange things in life, we simply discuss and observe them. This also lets new experiences present themselves to grab our attention.

SOME PEOPLE LOOK DIFFERENT NOW

As you grow and let go of baggage, be prepared to view people you know differently. In fact, it may be essential that you perceive them differently in order to embrace the new chapter you may or may not share with them. You gain clarity or insights about individuals in your life. You may decide to love some people from a distance.

YOU'RE OKAY

Change is essential in life. Keeping yourself grounded while giving your dreams permission to take flight keeps life fresh and interesting. It is okay that you feel different and have let some things go. It is okay to pursue new experiences and relationships. Others may or may not like it. However, time cannot be recaptured; therefore, you must spend it well.

CHALLENGES WILL CONTINUE THROUGHOUT LIFE

Challenges cycle throughout life and you can expect new ones to be around the corner. Some may be more compelling than others. You can get better at handling them, although you may still be blindsided at times. It helps to be more aware that life hands you surprises. Reacting with wisdom builds your confidence in handling situations. We can share our experiences and help others get through their own challenges. This makes the cycle purposeful.

EXHILARATION

Remember that people, achievements and experiences can exhilarate you. It is worth the risk. Stressful events are part of the mix.

My mother-in-law told me, "Stress makes you realize that you are still alive." That makes me smile. Know that many positive adventures remain out there, waiting for you. I cannot wait. Can you?

Carla Carroll, NMLS, CA BRE
Sr. Mortgage Banker, Author, Speaker
Diversified Capital Funding®
Positioning People Back into Homes

209-914-3753
ccarroll@divcap.net
www.divcap.net

Carla's 10 years of mortgage lending experience include banking, brokering and direct lending services. She combines this with over twenty years of high-tech experience, primarily with Fortune 500 companies, including Hewlett-Packard® Corp. Carla is a licensed senior loan officer and first obtained her real estate license in 2004. She works for Diversified Capital Funding.

Carla values community service, integrity, confidentiality, and the willingness to go the extra mile to find the best financial mortgage solution for her clients. She is committed to positively impacting the residential mortgage industry. Carla is enthusiastic about helping her clients realize their dreams.

Carla served on the board of directors of a non-profit organization in Tracy, California, for seven years. She served as president from 2008 to 2009 for Tracy's five clubs that serve youths. Carla has served as vice president of a local Business Networking International® group. In 2008, she co-founded All About Business, a networking organization in Tracy. Carla has authored and published more than twenty mortgage industry articles. She is currently a member of the Central Valley Association of Realtors, Women's Success Connection, Goldstar Referral Group, and the Tracy Business Networking Association.

The Heart of Shame

By Michelle Gesky, CRC, CLC, CHC

What is the heart of shame? For many, simply reading the word "shame" in print conjures negative connotations and feelings. I present to you a different perspective of shame. The heart of shame can be a place of strength and acceptance. It beats with your values, intuition and authenticity. It is an indicator that you are not aligned with who you are.

Shame is your authentic self, rising up to say *take notice*. It is drawing your attention to the misalignment between you and your actions or inactions. The heart of shame is the majesty of you. The authentically aligned you is using the uncomfortable experience of shame—as a tool—to communicate with you. This is meant to set you on a course to change your circumstance by re-aligning you with your values, purpose, intuition and authentic self.

Connotations or beliefs are often not the truth—especially when you are in the grips of the outer edge of an unhealthy shame paradigm. Unhealthy shame is like the undertow in the ocean pulling you in, under and away from the shores of the foundation of your heart and values. It undermines your ability to tap into the power of your authentic alignment and distorts your perception of yourself and your situation.

GETTING TO KNOW YOUR SHAME

When was the last time you experienced shame? Reflect on something that happened to you or someone you love that brought up feelings of shame. Can you remember what prompted it? Can you reflect on the emotions you experienced at the time? Unhealthy shame blocks authentic alignment. Taking the time to answer these questions is a courageous act that can bring you closer to claiming the authentically aligned you.

I encourage you to hold those moments of shame to the light, because there is a heart to shame. The question is whether it is healthy or unhealthy. If you can give yourself permission to face what shame is for you as an individual, then you can start to articulate and define it for yourself. Gaining clarity about what the word "shame" means to you is the first step to giving you the power to be authentic even when shame comes knocking on your door.

HEALTHY VERSUS UNHEALTHY SHAME

Shame has two guises: healthy and unhealthy. Although experiencing healthy shame can hurt inside, it can also transform your heart and how you feel about yourself if you listen to it, accept it, make different choices, and learn from what it communicates. It is a wake-up call that you are in a situation or paradigm that is not what you want to create.

The second kind of shame, the unhealthy shame, is inauthentic. It is what you learn from adults and society as a child. You held people's repeated judgements and beliefs as truths, rules, and regulations that governed you. Shame in this case is the historical voice and beliefs of your parents. If you experience yourself listening to the internal critical voice, you may be listening and unconsciously experiencing sadness and pain as your younger self, even though your body may physically be 42.

As your younger self, you absorb those experiences from childhood. You attach to the critical voice of shame hoping to be accepted and loved, and to learn the lesson from that voice so you do not make the mistake again. As an adult, even though intellectually you fear shame and want to quiet the critical self unconsciously, you do not want to un-attach from the judge, because the critical voice has been a parent to you and is familiar. It is your safety net. When you try to shut the critical voice off in your head, your subconscious young child within is still attached to the unhealthy shame. She is afraid to let go and, therefore, gets nowhere.

RESETTING YOUR SHAME BUTTON

To progress toward healthy shame is to become conscious of when you are subconsciously attached to criticism and to help your inner younger self to let go. Many people who have moved to their authentic, healthy heart of shame have used the following exercise to start untethering from their unhealthy shame:

Picture yourself when you were young and you felt shame. Take a moment to experience it. Add yourself into the picture as the adult holding your younger self's hand or wrapping your arms around the little you. Then speak out for your younger self as your adult self. Tell the unhealthy voice of shame that you do not need it right now and you will be responsible from now on. Tell the voice whatever you need to say to help your younger you un-attach. Perhaps you are telling the critical inner voice of the past that you are strong and wise or that it is has been hurtful. Acknowledge your feelings for both the adult you and the younger you as you speak to the inner critic. Then tell your younger self that she is loved and able to make her own choices. What do you feel when you finish the exercise? This brings you a step closer to the experience of healthy shame.

Taking the time to discover more about your personal shame may bring up resistance. Perhaps you do not want the feeling you get when looking within yourself. In a recent coaching session, Carol, a client, cried to me in anger, "I don't like the pain and the sadness. For me, I feel fear because I think I feel self-loathing when I'm ashamed. I just come away feeling depressed, small, and alone in my grief about who I am when I feel shame."

Like Carol, you may find that facing things you dislike about yourself may be difficult. You may feel ashamed of yourself when you look in the mirror and afraid of facing the emotions that come with that. When you experience unhealthy shame, it may feel like self-loathing, avoidance and unworthiness. It may feel like fear of abandonment, fear of looking bad, or fear of being wrong. You may feel humiliated and judged. You may suffer deep pain or feel anxious at the thought of having to face being confronted, found out, or exposed to someone. Worse yet, you may perceive yourself as being the mistake, rather than thinking, *I made a mistake, but I am not the mistake.*

Resetting your shame button by practicing the exercise above helps you un-attach from unhealthy paradigms and emotions and recognize them for the illusion of yourself that the unhealthy shame portrays.

Looking at examples from your own life, can you identify which shame you are living with or have lived with? All human beings are hard-wired with shame from infancy. At its best, shame helps us to learn, in a healthy way, when there is an opportunity to grow and mature. Shame is a program in your human operating system. It sounds an alarm in the form of an uncomfortable feeling when you are out of alignment with who you are in your heart, your soul or your spirit. It can be articulating that there is something you still need learn and grow from.

I can remember feeling shame after I did not defend my little brother from something that the neighborhood kids thought he did. Feeling shame was a healthy and positive thing for the seven-year-old me. It helped me see my behavior or lack of behavior for what it was and created a new path for me to take: to stand up and fight for my brother. The shame made me face what I knew from my childhood values. The authentic me would have stood up to the bullies to support my brother. My values were loyalty, truth-telling and love. When I did not act accordingly, the shame program in my operating system showed me the light. I was out of integrity with my values and not in authentic alignment with my young self. Shame assisted me in returning to the authentic me who loved and stood up for her brother. Once I had accepted the experience of that feeling and did not hold on to it, but instead used the shame to awaken to my authentic truth and take action, my early operating system then freed me from that shame. I had forgiven myself.

Think of your internal processes, both conscious and subconscious, as an operating system similar to a computer's. The operating system runs quietly in the background. Sometimes, programs in the operating system need to be updated. As an adult, you have the choice to use the new, updated operating system, or to trust the one installed in youth long ago by your parents, siblings, friends, community, church and school. If the thought of shame brings up feelings you would rather avoid, you may still be using your outdated shame program. Signs showing it is the old operating system include voices in your head saying things like *You shouldn't have, Now look what you've done, You should be seen and not heard, You are an idiot,* or *You are not good enough.* These voices are toxic and, over time, can cause you damage. Like a computer, bad coding may cause you to crash.

If the thought of shame brings tender feelings toward yourself for the times when you were ashamed, then chances are you are using an updated operating system.

The following short fable, *The Duck and the Moon,* illustrates the scenario of being stuck in an outdated paradigm in another way:

> *"A duck was once swimming along the river looking for fish.*
> *The whole day passed without her finding a single one. When night came she saw the moon reflected on the water,*
> *and thinking it was a fish she dove down to catch it. The other ducks saw her, and they all made fun of her.*
> *From that day the duck was so ashamed and so timid, that even when she did see a fish under water she would not try to catch it, and before long she died of hunger."*
> **—Leo Tolstoy, Russian novelist, short story writer, essayist, playwright and philosopher**

What happened to Tolstoy's duck is an example of shame gone awry. Have you ever left a room feeling uncomfortable or embarrassed because of something you did or did not do that may have hurt someone, or where you thought you damaged your own reputation? Perhaps you avoided attending a party because you felt ashamed, or did not throw your name into the hat to compete for something you wanted. Your old operating system may have been sending you messages that you were not enough, that you were inadequate, or that you would not be accepted.

People can be mean-spirited or judgmental. They can make you uncomfortable and act as if you are less than or unequal to them. It is not the truth. That is only their belief. If you have unhealthy shame installed by your old operating system, you may believe that you are the problem. Like the duck in Tolstoy's fable, you die a little. Your soul, your spirit and your authentic self becomes muted if you give up and persecute yourself.

Do not define yourself by your mistakes. You have control over your situation. In your new operating system, shame is a wake-up call. Healthy shame is a call to action toward who you truly are and what you want from your life. Realize you are a beautiful, whole, authentic, complete human being who can make mistakes and then correct them.

Allow healthy shame to guide you back to your authentic path and reroute you toward reaching your goals. It reminds you to listen to your intuition. It helps you understand the difference between others' judgments of you and the truth of who you are.

Shame also has fear attached to it. Healthy shame communicates to you, *Hold on, don't go there.* Unhealthy shame has a component of fear running through it. For example, fear is what we experience when we look in the mirror and it reflects back what we fear and not what actually exists. Fear is a part of survival and therefore is a part of our operating system. It also is a catalyst for shame.

*"It is not that you must be free from fear. The moment you
try to free yourself from fear is the moment you create resistance
against fear. What is needed, rather than running away or controlling
or suppressing or any other resistance, is understanding fear; that
means, watch it, learn about it, come directly into contact with it.
We are to learn about fear, not how to escape from it, not how to
resist it through courage and so on."*
—Krishnamurti, Indian speaker and writer

If we transpose what Krishnamurti said about fear to address shame, it can start to powerfully shift your relationship with the unhealthy heart of shame.

SHAME AND THE ANATOMY OF THE BRAIN

American society has long believed that talking about emotions is not helpful. We do not trust sharing about our experiences. We have fear around it. However, Dr. Mathew Leiberman, a neuroscientist, has researched the value of naming emotions. He found it maximizes cognitive ability. He also discovered that even using simple language to name emotions helps to quiet the arousal in our limbic system—the brain's emotional dashboard.

According to Dr Lieberman, suppressing emotions is costly and unhelpful. It is a high intensity job for your brain, and actually causes you to wastefully use up energy you might otherwise use to right your ship. Suppressing emotions also degrades your ability to recall information. The whole purpose of shame is to learn from your mistakes. Suppressing the emotions makes it harder for you to remember or learn. Talking about experiences of shame allows your brain to function optimally, remember more, and help you feel less pain.

An article in Choice magazine by Doug Rock, author of *Your Brain at Work,* published by Harper Collins in 2009, highlights that a quieter brain state makes the brain function better. The end result is that talking about your emotions is helpful because it dilutes the strong feelings around them. This means that when your shame indicator light comes on, it is a good idea to share your experience with someone you trust, or even talk it through with yourself. This lessens the uncomfortable emotions quickly.

SHAME AS YOUR GUIDE

Shame is the shepherd across the desert of your mistakes. Is your shepherd wise and gentle, yet firm, calling you out and upward, or is it judgmental, bullying and manipulative? Which one would you choose to guide you to your authentic self?

The human system is designed to have you thrive, not just survive. When you observe, understand and speak about your shame, it can help you learn to act on your values and intuition. This brings you into alignment with the authentic you. Understand that both operating systems are still in place within you. I encourage you to take the time to observe and identify which one is guiding your experience each time shame comes into play. This can help you listen for the message that is in alignment with the authentic you and move forward, lesson learned, free and powerful!

Michelle Gesky, CRC, CLC, CHC
Direct Impact Coaching & Training

914-471-5712
michelle.gesky@gmail.com
www.directimpactnow.org

Michelle Gesky is an advocate for creating extraordinary life experiences for her clients. She explores their passions, dreams and goals, and digs into what matters most to them. This creates incredible success with love, laughter and deep curiosity.

Michelle is a Certified Relationship, Leadership, and Health and Wellness Coach. She has twenty years of experience working for training companies and corporations to train and coach employees within organizations. Michelle's skills include individual and organizational assessments, training, executive and personal coaching and development, strategic planning, communications, and presenting and designing powerful workshops to create breakthroughs in relationship to self and others.

After years dedicated to business professionals in the corporate arena, from Fortune 500 companies to small and mid-sized companies, Michelle is now living her passion in her own thriving business by empowering others to do the same. She is an intuitive, compassionate transformational coach committed to helping her clients live authentic, purpose-filled, joyful lives full of possibility. She has worked with thousands of people from all walks of life.

More
Authentic Alignment

Now that you have been inspired by our stories and have learned a wide variety of tips, techniques and strategies to achieve authentic alignment, the next step is to take action. Get started applying what you have learned in the pages of this book.

We want you to know that we are here to help and inspire you to meet your personal objectives. The following pages list our geographical locations. Regardless of where we are located, many of us provide a variety of services over the phone or through webinars, and we welcome the opportunity to travel to your location or invite you to ours.

You can find out more about each of us by reading our bios at the end of our chapters, or by visiting our websites listed there and on the following pages. When you call us, let us know you have read our book. We are here to serve you on your *amazing* journey to authentic alignment!

Geographical Listings for
Authentic Alignment

California

Linda Ashley	www.ashleybiz.com
Carla Carroll	www.divcap.net
Dot Claire	www.dotclaire.com
Rayna Lumbard	www.innersuccess.com
Katie Macks	www.getyourglowon.us
Patti Martin	www.createyourchangenow.com
Christy Moore	www.moorejoycoaching.com
Shannon Murray	www.shensounds.com
Paula E. Pacheco	www.paulapacheco.com
Vicki Takeuchi Wynne	www.vickiwynne.com

Minnesota

Kecia Hayslett	www.keciahayslett.com

New York

Michelle Gesky	www.directimpactnow.org

Texas

Maria Antonieta Gomez	www.yourmagdream.com

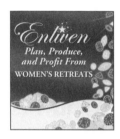

Attend Enliven...

. . .you will learn to plan, produce and profit from women's retreats and events, while inspiring women, and sharing your special gifts and talents. In this two-day live event you will learn to create connections that matter, camaraderie, and community of like minded women who share your passion and purpose. You will discover so many ways to bring women together and walk away with a clear plan to monetize your passion with retreats and events. You will get questions answered as you learn to make your events memorable and uplifting, and how to bring awesome value to the participants.

Join Caterina as she shares her seven step system for retreat and event success, and how she has multiplied her investment. Go to enlivenprogram.com to learn more and download your free audio on "How to Host Your Own Successful Retreat." Enter this promo code when you register to get a special *Authentic Alignment* discount! Code ENAA.

You're Invited...

...to join us for any of our Sought After Speaker Summits!

Do you have a message you want to share?
Are you ready to improve your speaking skills?
Have you seen how much influence people who speak have?
Would you like be a sought-after speaker?

In one weekend you can develop your public speaking skills and be loud and proud about the value you bring. Join us for our next live event at: www.soughtafterspeaker.com

Because you are savvy enough to pick up this book we have a gift for you. Enter coupon code SASVIP50 for a 50% discount on your registration. Attend this event and watch how your social status climbs!

Get Published with
Thrive Publishing™

THRIVE Publishing™ develops books for experts who want to share their knowledge with more and more people. We provide our co-authors with a proven system, professional guidance and support, thereby producing quality, multi-author, how-to books that uplift and enhance the personal and professional lives of the people they serve.

We know that getting a book written and published is a huge undertaking. To make that process as easy as possible, we have an experienced team with the resources and know-how to put a quality, informative book in the hands of our co-authors quickly and affordably. Our co-authors are proud to be included in THRIVE Publishing™ books because these publications enhance their business missions, give them a professional outreach tool and enable them to communicate essential information to a wider audience.

You can find out more about our upcoming book projects at
www.thrivebooks.com.

Contact us to discuss how we can work together
on *your* book project.

Phone: **415-668-4535**
email: **info@thrivebooks.com**

Other Books from
THRIVE Publishing

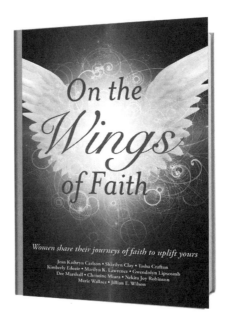

For more information on
On the Wings of Faith, visit:
www.thrivebooks.com/store

Other Books from
THRIVE Publishing

For more information on
Catch Your Star, visit:
www.thrivebooks.com/store

Other Books from
THRIVE Publishing

For more information on
Power to Change, visit:
www.thrivebooks.com/store

Other Books from
THRIVE Publishing

For more information on
Make Your Connections Count, visit:
www.thrivebooks.com/store

Other Books from
THRIVE Publishing

For more information on
Get Organized Today, visit:
www.thrivebooks.com/store

Other Books from
THRIVE Publishing

For more information on
Incredible Life, visit:
www.thrivebooks.com/store

Notes

Notes

For more copies of this book,
Authentic Alignment
contact any of the co-authors or visit
www.thrivebooks.com/store